A
Year of
Forest School

Outdoor Play and Skill-building
Fun for Every Season

Jane Worroll & Peter Houghton

WATKINS
Sharing Wisdom Since 1893

A Year of Forest School
Jane Worroll and Peter Houghton

First published in the UK and USA in 2018 by
Watkins, an imprint of Watkins Media Limited
Unit 11, Shepperton House
89-93 Shepperton Road
London N1 3DF

enquiries@watkinspublishing.com

Development Editor: Fiona Robertson
Managing Editor: Daniel Hurst
Editor: Victoria Godden
Art Editor: Karen Smith
Commissioned artwork: Peter Houghton
Production: Uzma Taj

A CIP record for this book is
available from the British Library

ISBN: 978-1-78678-131-4

10 9 8

Typeset in Archer
Colour reproduction by XY Digital
Printed in Slovenia

www.watkinspublishing.com

PUBLISHER'S NOTE:
Some activities in this book, for example
those involving fire or cutting tools, may be
dangerous if instructions are not followed
precisely. Always follow manufacturers'
instructions when using tools. Wild foods
such as berries can be poisonous, so eat only
what you can identify as safe. Adults need to
assess each child's capabilities and supervise
any potentially dangerous activity at all times.
Watkins Media Limited, or any other persons
who have been involved in working on this
publication, cannot accept responsibility for
any injury, illness or damages that result from
participating in the activities in this book.

CONTENTS

Introduction

Since ancient times, human beings have marked the progress of time by observing the passing of the seasons, each of which deeply influenced their lives, as they still do today for people who work closely with the land. As the months go by, nature offers us all new wonders to remind us of the ever-turning cycle of life, from the transforming magic of the first winter snowfall to the beauty of spring blossom, from the warmth of summer sunlight on the skin to the scrunch of fallen autumn leaves underfoot. These are just some of the joys that nature shares with us, connecting us to the cycles of the Earth as it did for our ancestors.

At our own Forest School groups we see how each season has a rhythm all its own that in turn affects the mood and energy of children and adults alike. After the rush of life that invigorates and awakens us in spring, we feel ourselves slowing down to savour the more relaxed pace of summertime. Autumn, with its shortening days and deepening colours, brings on another change of mood, with all the excitement of kicking leaves; then comes winter, a season of crisp fresh air, running around and wrapping up warm until spring when the cycle begins once again.

Today our modern lives are often estranged from the natural world and what should be an inherent connection may feel more like something we need to rediscover and reclaim. It is well documented that today's children, especially those in developed countries, are playing outside far less than their parents and grandparents did. These societal changes are being partly fuelled by a combination of disappearing open spaces, increasing traffic and the lure of indoor technology and virtual reality as well as heightened parental expectations of what a "safe" environment looks like. But while the outdoors may seem like a dangerous option these days, it's a lack of outside activity that is the primary cause of obesity – one of the biggest threats to the health of our children today. This loss of freedom to roam, coupled with the increasing pressures on children such as target-driven school life, 24-hour social media and, for those in the city, cognitive fatigue from constant urban stimulation, has also resulted in serious mental health issues arising among 5–16 year olds.

Most of us instinctively recognize the many ways that being outside in a natural environment can enrich our lives: we might find we sleep more deeply after spending time walking outdoors or notice a lift in mood after breathing in a few lungfuls of fresh air. Studies have highlighted a multitude of health benefits to being outside: sunlight and soil micro-organisms boost the body's levels of serotonin, the chemical linked to feelings of wellbeing, while Vitamin D, essential for bone and muscle health, is also provided by the sun's rays. Running across uneven terrain and climbing trees helps children develop muscle strength and become more coordinated. Mental health professionals also acknowledge the benefits of maintaining a relationship with nature. In ecotherapy, for example, nature has been found to be a restorative influence in the lives of patients who engage, without judgement or artificial time limits, in outdoor activities such as conservation work and gardening. Forest School is an inclusive grassroots movement that can help to redress some of the issues affecting our modern-day lives – it aims to connect participants with nature and offers opportunities to develop and grow away from the indoors, busy streets and pervasive technology, which, though not all bad, are now a constant presence in our lives.

WHAT IS FOREST SCHOOL?

Forest School is defined by the Forest School Association as "an inspirational process that offers *all* learners regular opportunities to achieve and develop confidence and self-esteem through hands-on learning experiences in a woodland or natural environment with trees." Forest School sessions are now offered in a huge range of settings from city parks to rural forests, by many different providers including mainstream schools, specialist outdoor kindergartens, holiday and after-school clubs and agencies countering addiction and social exclusion, but all have this in common: they take place in a natural environment where the qualified leader aims to provide a nurturing space that supports the learner's wellbeing. The activities offered provide different experiences that can help foster traits such as resilience, confidence and emotional intelligence that will support the learner throughout their lives. Within this framework the participants are given ownership over their journey to follow their interests and develop their own learning at their own pace.

At Forest School, children run and make a noise, get their hands dirty and are exposed to manageable risk (essential for healthy development). To fully embed learning and develop a sense of community, Forest School sessions have a high adult-to-child ratio and take place, with the same group, on a regular, long-term basis.

We use a variety of locations for our own Forest School, and repeated visits make each of these sites familiar to our groups. This helps children feel a sense of belonging and gain confidence by allowing them to get to know each other and the boundaries (both physical and behavioural), as well as where their basic needs can be met – where they will eat and where they can shelter (in dens or under tarps, for example), the location of the toilets and hand-washing facilities. From this basis, interests can be freely followed and deeper learning of practised skills explored and mastered. Unlike tightly regulated and confined school classrooms, the open surroundings of Forest School sites allows children greater personal control over social interactions, as there is freedom for all to move around and consciously choose the space they occupy, which helps relationships build in a more relaxed atmosphere.

Visiting a Forest School throughout the year, groups see how "their" space changes, and they develop an intimate understanding of each season and the effects of the weather on a natural environment. We have noticed how, during the warmer months, the children's attention is always more drawn toward the animals and plants that surround them. In colder months, we find it is the elements that take precedence: they love jumping into and cracking ice-covered puddles, making fire and leaning into strong winds. Each season provides wonderful moments of discovery and interaction that have a positive, lasting effect on every child's sense of belonging and stewardship over the various Forest School sites.

PLAYING THROUGH THE YEAR

In this book we offer a wide range of Forest School activities to
tie in with spring, summer, autumn and winter. In choosing the
activities, we were inspired by what nature offers in each season, as
well as by the festivities celebrated at different times of year, and,
of course, the weather. It's in spring, for example, that brambles are
at their most pliable and the nettles start shooting up, so now is
the perfect time to make cordage from bramble vines (see page 27)
and soup from the tender nettle tips (see page 18). In summer, the
intuition game (see page 66) allows children to be still and relax
in the heat of the day and get a sense of their intuitive awareness
(like that of the creatures all around them); while making and using
walking sticks (see page 80) will encourage them to tap into the
ease and carefree happiness of being in nature on a warm summer's
day. In autumn, children can collect fallen leaves of every hue and
make a rainbow from them (see page 114), as well as gather apples
and nuts to bake over a fire (see page 120). And winter is a perfect
time for observing animal tracks left in snow or mud (see page 144),
as well as warming up around a fire and making charcoal sticks for
outdoor art (see page 158). From our own Forest School we know
how coming together around a fire can create a joyful sense of
community and transform what could otherwise be a cold, grey day
into a place that's fun and welcoming.

For each season we have also designed a day out that combines
a range of activities – energetic games, calmer crafts and social
tasks (such as foraging, cooking, fire-making or den-building).
This could be used as the basis of a party, playdate or some other
type of extended Forest School session.

BUILDING A SESSION

This book is not a replacement for the full experience of going to Forest School (if your child has not done this already, please do consider trying it out!), but it does offer a taster of some of the wonderful Forest School activities we use. It's written for anyone who wants to spend more time outdoors with the children in their care, whether you are a parent, a guardian, a teacher or a youth worker; we also hope it will be a handy resource for Forest School leaders. Whoever you are, the aim is to emulate a Forest School leader by being fully present, enthusiastic, encouraging, inspiring and observant, helping out with an activity when needed and demonstrating new skills when the time's right, but allowing the learning to be led by the child. A Forest School leader will also reflect on how each session went for each child and encourage children to reflect on their own experiences. This information shapes future sessions with the aim of providing opportunities for each child to grow and develop as a whole – physically, mentally, emotionally, spiritually and socially. Learning outcomes are provided within each activity and may be useful for planning.

Each seasonal chapter offers a range of different activities, some high energy, some requiring more focused participation. The more familiar you become with the activities, the easier it will be to switch between them as needed. For example, you may have a group where not all the children know each other. It is a warm spring day and the energy level is high, so a team game (such as Mammoth, Hunter, Mouse, see page 32) would be a fantastic ice breaker and way to start. Once some of that initial energy has been released, the children's attention can then be turned to crafts, which lend themselves well to the warmer seasons. Their nimble fingers could be put to work making a sistrum (see page 36), for example, that can later be used for a group sing-song, further building a sense of trust and community, and shared happy memories for all.

In Forest School, each session has a clear beginning and ending. Before we start, the boundaries of the play area and the rules regarding safety and care for each other and the environment are established with the whole group. We also point out where the toilets are, where food will be kept, where we can wash our hands and shelter. In groups, it can be helpful to sit in a circle during this opening time, taking it in turns to share thoughts and feelings.

You can also use this time to gauge the mood and energy levels of the children before deciding on the most appropriate activity to do first. You can either ask them directly how they feel (especially if you are looking after young children, just one child or a small group) or, with larger numbers (especially older kids), you could suggest they rate their feelings on a scale of 1 to 10. This often encourages children to share their feelings. The same technique can be used at the end of the session, when we like to round off the day by inviting the children to share how they now feel and provide an opportunity for them to reflect on their experiences. As well as helping the children to process the day, this encourages them to play an active role in their own learning. And these discussions are a fantastic way of allowing you to gain insight into what worked and what could be adjusted about each activity, providing a valuable guide for future sessions. Remember, however, these are only invitations to share and some children may be too shy at first.

A BRIEF GUIDE

Before you try out an activity, bear the following points in mind:

→ The activities are suitable for a wide age range (from pre-school children up to about the age of 12), with a different level of adult guidance needed for different age groups. Assess the individual capabilities of each child before you start and adjust accordingly.

→ For each activity we've suggested a list of kit, but also bring a first-aid kit and hand-cleaning supplies, if not available nearby.

→ If an activity requires more than one child to take part, the ideal number is always stated in the activity.

→ Activities can take place in all weathers (except high winds in woods), so make sure children have suitable clothes for the weather – waterproof clothing and suitable boots can make the difference between a fun day out and a miserable one!

→ Make sure there are enough adults present to allow children to engage in achievable, challenging activities in a safe space.

→ Demonstrate any tricky techniques at the start of each activity, then let the children attempt each step, offering positive encouragement, and only assisting if required.

→ Let kids work things out for themselves, if they want to. We've designed the step-by-step instructions and diagrams to be as simple and easily grasped as possible.

Play Safe

Any activity that involves foraging for wild food, tool use or fire does contain an element of risk, but by referring back to the guidelines below as you work through this book and implementing the basic safety procedures outlined, you will be more than ably equipped to avoid any potential mishaps. Above all, the activities in this book are designed to be interactive, educational, inspirational – and fun.

TOOL USE

Whether an adult is using tools alone or children are handling them under adult supervision, follow manufacturers' guidelines and the safety procedures outlined below.

The age at which children are able to use tools under adult supervision varies, so assess each child individually. If you are confident that the child is capable, allow tool use. However, close adult supervision is still required. As a general rule (apart from knife work when one-on-one is advisable), have one adult watching a maximum of four capable older kids and a higher adult-to-child ratio with younger ones for safety.

For extra protection when using tools, a gardening glove can be worn on helper hands but not on the hand holding the tool (as this can lessen the grip). Stress that all tools must go back to an adult when they're no longer being used, at which point they should be stored out of the way with all security catches on as necessary.

Before embarking on using any tool, ensure a capable adult
has demonstrated its use in full to every member of your group
following the guide below:

→ Tell everyone the name of the tool that they will be using and
   what it is used for.

→ Show everyone the cover (if it has one), how to take it off and
   put it on or how to open it and close it.

→ Show them the handle and the cutting edge of the tool.

→ Demonstrate how each tool works.

→ Show how best to position hands in order to use it safely and
   cleanly, and how to carry it safely: covered or closed at your side,
   with the blade pointing toward the floor, and no running!

→ Explain about the safe working zone: this is a circle the diameter
   of the tool used and the tool user's outstretched arms. If anyone
   (apart from your partner) comes inside the circle, tool use should
   stop until the zone is empty again.

How to use a sheath knife

It's worth going over the instructions for a sheath knife in detail, as
this is an advanced tool, and is used often in this book. Show the
knife to everyone, pointing out the blade cover and handle. Show
how, by placing one gloved hand at the tip end of the blade, you are
able to pull the cover off and then clip it back on. Once off again,

point to the blade and its cutting edge. Explain that it is a great tool for carving wood. If possible, sit off the ground, on a stump for example, and with a gloved hand put the wood you are carving to one side of your body. With the knife in the other ungloved hand, cut the wood away from your body. Point out that you always carve away from your body and have no limbs underneath or hands in front of the blade. If sitting cross-legged on the floor, either carve to one side of your body or place elbows on knees and carve away from your body here – again, making sure there are no limbs underneath or in front of the blade. (This technique also works with potato peelers and is good practice as a precursor to knife work.)

FORAGING

Being able to positively identify edible wild foods is vital as many plants are poisonous. Always take a field guide with you or use your smartphone to access a website with pictures of edible plants, and choose to forage wild foods that can be easily identified. Always check if any of your group have any allergies before foraging for wild food, particularly nuts. Always pick wild food away from pollution sources such as roads, dog-walking spots and sprayed farm margins.

Conservation

We share this planet with many species who rely on the natural larder as their only source of food. With this in mind, think sustainably, spread your foraging over as large an area as possible, and never over-harvest or uproot any plant. Follow local regulations about what you can and cannot pick and, if necessary, check with the landowner first.

FIRE SAFETY

↓ Before lighting a fire, check the ground conditions: never light a fire on peaty soil (it is flammable), and remember that porous rocks can also explode. Push any flammable material away from the fire area, and dowse this area with water in very dry weather. Check for and remove any trip hazards.

↓ Keep the fire small and usable.

↓ Do not burn wood that gives off toxic fumes.

↓ Before using the fire, tie back all long hair and secure any dangling jewellery and clothing.

FIRE SAFETY KIT
Always have the following items close by when working with fire: an open container of water; a fire blanket, for first aid if needed and to put out the fire; welding gloves or equivalent fire-resistant material for handling hot items.

↓ An adult must supervise lit fires at all times.

↓ A metre (yard) square frame of logs/branches around the fire site helps to contain the fire and marks out the fire boundary that is not to be crossed.

↓ No running, pushing or games should take place around the fire site.

↓ Only those cooking or sitting should be around the fire site. To limit accidents and increase balance and stability, have anyone cooking on or tending the fire kneel on one knee.

↓ Extinguish the fire properly before leaving, let it die down and then spread the ashes out and douse with water until cool to touch. For temporary fire sites, either spread the cold ash around, bury it or take it off site so that you leave no trace.

Spring

As the days become longer and warmer and winter loosens its grip over the land, animals awaken from their hibernation, the bare earth is covered with fresh green shoots, and birdsong fills the air. From ancient times, spring has been recognized as a season of beginnings, of renewal and rebirth.

Spring injects new energy and life into nature, awakening and transforming the land and its inhabitants. As buds and blossom emerge, we see the irrepressible energy of spring bubbling up in our groups, giving each child a renewed sense of curiosity and desire to participate. Despite an occasional chill in the air, there is a visible willingness to spend more time outside. It's wonderful to see them notice the flashing bright-yellow wings of brimstone butterflies as they sail through the air, a blackbird's alarm call or the purple-blue hues of bluebells appearing in places that seemed empty during winter's sleep.

At this time of the year, we make sure our Forest School activities make the most of this newfound energy and curiosity. Whether it be foraging for plants or joining in with the songs of the season, the activities found within this section are guaranteed to tap into this exploration of new life and the wonderful, transformational joy of spring.

NETTLE SOUP

Foraging is a fantastic way to teach children where food comes from and how it grows in the wild. The discovery that some of nature's wild offerings are edible, and come and go as the year progresses, connects children to the environment and the rhythm of the natural world.

This activity is filled with fun. Finding the right plant can take you on a long walk, many bugs and plants catching attention along the way and triggering a child's focus, communication and curiosity in the world around them.

Nettles (*Urtica dioica*) are one of the most recognizable plants – mostly because, once stung, we try our best to avoid them! Although it doesn't sound like a good idea to eat anything that has the word "stinging" in its name, nettles are full of nutrients. Gathering and cooking wild food combines multiple skills in one task: plant identification; sustainability; risk assessing; hygiene; fine motor skills, such as chopping; planning; sharing; and discussions on nutrition, which can develop a sense of independence, raising self-esteem. As long as you're careful, nettles can be picked and eaten like any other vegetable – in fact, in any recipe where you'd usually use spinach or kale, so feel free to play around. Here we will use them for one of our favourites – nettle soup.

LOCATION	Woodland, hedgerows, river banks, parks, wastelands, gardens
AGE GROUP	6 years + (for tasting, any age!)
LEARNING ABOUT ...	Species identification ⊕ fine motor skills ⊕ nature connections ⊕ nutrition ⊕ communication ⊕ sharing ⊕ risk management ⊕ curiosity ⊕ self-esteem ⊕ independence ⊕ sustainability ⊕ focus
SAFETY	An anti-histamine cream can be useful for any accidental stings!

KIT

- → A basket or bag
- → Gardening gloves (one pair per person)
- → Camp fire kit (see page 89) and fire safety kit (see page 15) or camping stove
- → Soap and water

- → Large plastic bowl
- → Scissors
- → Chopping board
- → Chopping knife
- → Heavy-bottomed pan
- → Wooden spoon
- → Ladle, spoons, bowls or cups for soup

INGREDIENTS (to serve 4)

- → ½ carrier bag of nettle tops (if not available locally)
- → 1 clove garlic
- → 1 large onion
- → 2 large potatoes
- → 2 tbsp olive oil or 50g (2oz) butter
- → 1 vegetable or

- chicken stock cube
- → 150ml (¼ pint) single cream
- → 1 litre/1¾ pint bottle of water
- → Salt and pepper
- → Crusty loaf of bread or dampers (see page 164, optional)

Get ready

This is a great outdoor cooking
activity but the soup can also be
finished indoors and blended until
smooth, if you prefer. To avoid stings, tell
the children in advance to wear clothes that
cover their arms and legs. Before you set off, show everyone what
a nettle looks like. Take some time to discuss the important role
nettles play in nature, and the host of insects and animals that rely
on them for food and shelter. Remind everyone that we should only
forage what we need, making sure plants can continue to grow, and
to never uproot them.

Get set

Head off to your chosen nettle-picking spot, taking a bag or basket
for collecting the nettles in. Once the children have located a good
clump of nettles, demonstrate how to pluck off the small leaves at
the top of the plant, while wearing gardening gloves. Explain that
it's these tender leaves that are needed to make soup.

Go!

Now it's time for everyone to don gardening gloves and start
foraging! Keep going until you've collected enough leaves (about
half a carrier bag full). Then, either return to your indoor area or
prepare your camp fire (see page 89) or camping stove. Once hands
are washed, children can clean the nettles in a bowl filled with cold
water, with a little salt added. Tip them in and swoosh them around
a little, then leave them there for 10 minutes to give all the bugs a
chance to leave. Then, wearing gloves, pick up the nettles and trim

away any remaining stems with scissors. Finely slice the nettles on a chopping board. Peel and chop the garlic, onions and potatoes. Place your pan on the heat (wearing fire-resistant gloves for camp fires) and warm the butter or oil. Add the onion, garlic and potatoes and fry, stirring, for around 4 minutes. Now add your nettles, letting them cook for a couple of minutes (this will remove all the stinging hairs). Next add the water. Once boiling, add your stock cube. Boil for a further 15 minutes or until the potatoes are cooked. Season, then stir in the cream. Older children can often manage the cooking stage themselves, with supervision, but younger children may require a little more assistance. Ladle the soup into bowls or cups and serve with a slice of bread if you'd like, or with dampers (see page 164) – delicious either way!

Endings

Did the foragers like looking for wild food? If yes, why? Do they think they could spot nettles again? Remind them that picking wild food can be dangerous and they should always have someone with them who knows which plants are safe. How did they avoid the nettle stings? Why do they think nettles sting? Just as it stops them touching the leaves, these hairs protect them from animals – only hardy goats with tough tongues will eat them fresh! Many insects count on this protection and will lay their eggs on the plant. Some of these are beautiful butterflies, whose caterpillars love to feast

 on nettles. Talk about the sustainable use of resources and the importance of leaving some plants for other species and future generations.

WOOD-COOKIE MAN

Spring is the season of birth, renewal and transformation, so is the ideal time to transform a piece of wood into something new. In this activity, children get to join in with the ancient tradition of creating human-like figures – something that people have been doing for millennia! Decorating the wood-cookie man as they see fit, the children imbue it with its own set of characteristics and unique personality.

This activity pulls together a number of skills and opportunities to develop them. Firstly, the right type of wood has to be found, focusing a child's attention and connecting them to the environment. The process of cutting, drilling and piecing together the wooden character develops fine motor skills as well as the opportunity to practise safe tool use, patience, perseverance and determination. Working with 3D shapes taps into mathematical understanding, while creativity is fully employed as they lose themselves in the colour, shape and texture, and create a character for the wood-cookie man. As they envisage personality and actions for the character, they can work through their own inner thoughts and feelings. This work brings about a real sense of pride, as well as a sense of community as conversations ripple through the group. The play that unfolds is magical and full of enthusiasm.

LOCATION	Woodland is ideal as it provides the materials needed as well as a multi-layered environment for imaginative play. If you have collected the materials beforehand, any outdoor space will do.
AGE GROUP	4 years +
LEARNING ABOUT ...	Focus ❀ nature connections ❀ risk assessment ❀ tool use ❀ fine motor skills ❀ patience ❀ perseverance ❀ determination ❀ mathematics ❀ art ❀ tree identification ❀ creativity ❀ imagination ❀ communication ❀ achievement ❀ pride ❀ sensory experiences
KIT	→ Hand-held folding saw → Palm drill → Gardening gloves (one pair per person) → Permanent marker pens → Pipe cleaners of various colours → Scissors → String (optional) → Secateurs (optional)
SAFETY	See note on using tools safely on pages 12–14.

Get ready

Look for a fallen tree trunk or stump to provide a solid prop
for sawing and drilling. This will become your work space. Talk
through the safety aspects of using a hand-held saw and a palm
drill. Show how to unfold the saw, its cutting edge and how to close
it. Show the palm drill, indicating its handle and drill bit.

Find a rot- and preferably knot-free branch, roughly as long
as an adult's arm and about 4cm (1½in) in diameter. This will be
the head. Find another branch, this time roughly 5–6cm (2–2½in) in
diameter, for the body. Use fallen branches if you can, but if cutting
from a tree, get the landowner's permission and make a clean cut in
front of the branch bark collar or ridge to protect the tree. An adult
or older, capable child can do this.

Get set

Demonstrate how to cut a wood cookie. Prop the smaller branch
up against the log or tree stump. Kneel down in front of the branch
(this is a steady position that ensures all limbs are out of harm's
way), put a gardening glove on your free (non-cutting) hand and
use this hand (and if necessary your knee) to hold still the lower
side of the branch – the end that is not being cut. To protect your
free hand (the non-cutting hand), place it roughly 15cm (6in) away
from the cutting edge. Saw off the end of the branch to create a flat
surface. Then move the saw 1.5–2cm (½–¾in) along the branch and
cut off another section. This disc is your wood cookie!

Move the branch out of the way and put the disc on top of the
supportive surface. Hold the disc still with your gloved hand and
use the palm drill to make a hole through the cookie, close to
the edge. Explain that this will be the cookie man's head and the
hole you've made will allow us to attach it to his body. Repeat the
process with the larger branch, but this time drill five holes around
the edge of the cookie. One to attach the body to the head, then the
remaining four will be for arms and legs. Using pipe cleaners, piece
together your wood-cookie man.

Go!

Sawing It's time for the kids to have a go! If working with one adult per child, the adult braces and secures the branch, while the child kneels down, takes hold of the handle with both hands, and saws.

If you have a group of older children, you can ask two wearing gloves to kneel down facing one another to brace and steady the branch. The third person sawing can grasp the handle of the saw with both hands (no gloves) to cut the cookie. If working with younger children, it may be safer to hold the branch for them, but watch them closely and judge for yourself.

Drilling An adult needs to hold the cookie steady in a gloved hand as the child uses the palm drill to bore the holes near the edge. If older children feel they would like to try this alone, holding their own cookie as they drill, let them have a go, but make sure they are under adult supervision. Now put the tools safely away.

Decorating and attaching Now it's time to put the wood-cookie man together. Have the children lay the various pieces out so that the hole in the head lines up with the top hole in the body. Explain that this will be where they put a pipe cleaner, representing the wood-cookie man's neck. With this in mind, the children can now use the marker pens to bring their character to life, drawing eyes, a mouth and clothes on the wood – or whatever inspires them.

Once the designing has finished, let the children choose five coloured pipe cleaners: one for the neck, two for the arms and two for the legs. Colour may be important here, so give them options to choose from. Now have them thread one pipe cleaner between the head and neck, twisting it to secure. If it's too long, a section can be cut off with scissors. Do the same for the arms and legs, but this time they can be as long as they like. Welcome, wood-cookie man!

The great thing about pipe cleaners is there is no knot-tying for small children to tackle and they can grab onto things like branches during wood-cookie man's adventures. But, if older children fancy taking it one stage further, they can use secateurs to cut sticks for arms and legs, drilling holes and tying them onto the body with either pipe cleaners or string. They could use one stick for each limb or make it even more puppet-like by using two small sticks per limb – attaching them together at the elbow and knee respectively before attaching them all to the body.

Endings

If they are happy to do so, you could ask each child to explain who their wood-cookie characters are. Do they have any special powers or skills? Are they from Earth or elsewhere? Do they have a name? Ask the group which parts of the construction process they found difficult, and which parts they found easy. Now would be a good opportunity to have the children go through the safety points of using tools as they come up in the discussion. You could talk about how our ancestors across time from many different cultures have made all sorts of wooden figures. The oldest discovered, the Shigir Idol, is thought to be 11,000 years old!

BRAMBLE CORDAGE

**Whether for constructing dens
or incorporating into artworks,
our Forest School groups are
always asking us for string or cord.
In spring we can show the children
that they need look no further than their
immediate surroundings for this useful resource.**

Brambles (*Rubus fruiticosus*) are abundant in parks and forests.
Children are often familiar with this plant as they love to feast on
the fruits in summertime; the look of delight that crosses their faces
upon finding out it can be used to make cord is priceless! Brambles
produce new shoots each spring which are pliable and produce
good cord, making this season the ideal time for this activity.

We are always mindful to leave no trace after a Forest School
session. One of the best things about having the children make
their own bramble cordage is that it comes from the natural
environment and will eventually break down and return to the
soil. Understanding these processes and when and how to harvest
builds nature connections and an understanding of sustainability.
Hiking to find brambles, working safely and using tools develops
risk management and fine and gross motor skills. Creating the cord
requires focus, perseverance and patience. Once made, there is a
sense of achievement, independence and pride, raising self-esteem.
The cord can be used in many ways and if desired left on site; it's
perfect for dens and art that take dedication to create!

LOCATION	Parks, wasteland, heath, woodlands – most habitats with the exception of pine forests.
AGE GROUP	7 years +
LEARNING ABOUT ...	Tool use ❁ safety and risk management ❁ plant identification ❁ sustainability ❁ nature connections ❁ being active ❁ gross and fine motor skills ❁ focus ❁ creativity ❁ perseverance ❁ patience ❁ natural processes ❁ confidence ❁ independence ❁ transferable skills and ideas
KIT	→ Thick gardening gloves (one pair per person) → Secateurs → Sturdy stick as wide as your forearm (if none on the ground) → Potato peelers → Water for sprinkling cord (optional) → Cut section of bramble (optional)

Get ready

Make sure that everyone in the group knows what brambles look like and explain that you'll be turning the vines into cord, which can be used for all the things they would usually use string for. Explain that, being organic itself, this cordage can be left in the natural environment. To avoid scratches, tell the children in advance to wear clothes that cover their legs, and boots. Head off together to find your bramble bushes.

Get set

Once you have found your brambles, find some sticks for bashing the vines and a large log or tree stump that can be used to lay the vines across. Lay out all the equipment needed and explain that you will only be taking from nature what's necessary for the activity.

Put on gardening gloves, explain the safety rules for secateurs (see pages 12–14) and show the group how to use them. Explain that you will be using young fresh bramble vines as these green stalks are more pliable and have softer thorns. Check to ensure there are no nesting birds and, if clear, choose a length of vine from the outer edge of the bush and cut off as close to the base as possible (around 2m/6½ft is a good length for short arms to work with). For every child using secateurs, there must be one adult supervising.

Go!

Stripping Show how to remove the thorns and leaves by running a gloved hand from the tip of the vine to the base. This direction is best as brambles have backwards-facing thorns so your hand is less likely to get snagged. The ones near the base may be too tough to remove like this. If this is the case, you can use your hand-held stick to work them off.

Bramble stems have an inner and outer layer of bark: the outer layer is dark green; the inner, a light green, softer layer that lies around the central pith. It's the fibres from this inner bark that we are after. Lay the

29

vine on the floor and use the edge of a potato peeler (and not the blade) to scrape away the outer bark (giving the group directions for safe use, see pages 12–14). Do this gently to keep the softer light green fibres just below it intact.

Separating To separate the light green fibres from the central pith, place your vine on your stump or log and start to gently bash it with your stick, turning it around as you move toward the top of the stem. Now gently pull the stringy, translucent, whitish-green fibres away from the pith. Once you have your fibres, tease them apart into five even strands. If it's a warm day and the fibres start to dry out, sprinkle on some water to dampen them.

Twisting Take one strand and fold it in two, keeping one side roughly 15cm (6in) longer than the other (this shorter side will allow more fibres to be fed in when needed). Twist the strand at the fold a few turns, to form a tight, twisted loop. Lay the two strands across your thighs, and with your left hand hold the twisted loop, letting the other strands fall across to the outside of your leg. With your right hand, take the strand furthest away from your body and twist a small section away from you. Once twisted, wrap it across the strand that is closest to your body and move your left thumb and forefinger along to this overlapped part of your cord, pinching it to hold it in place.

Repeat this process along the strands, keeping it as tight as possible as you go. If the strand runs out or

becomes thin, add another strand to keep the cord long and strong. Try to pick a fibre that matches the thickness of the fibres that you already have, as this will keep your cord even in size. To add it in, simply take your new fibre and twist it together with the section that is running out, making this twist roughly 15cm (6 in) long. Once twisted together, simply carry on like before along the strands until you come to the end. Your cord is now complete.

Now it's the kids' turn! Let them work out which vine is best, and check everyone is clear on safety and techniques by having them tell you what they should be doing. Allow everyone to start making their cord, guiding and helping only when necessary.

Endings

Once complete, the children will be bursting with pride and you may find that they want to put their cord to use. What might they want to use their cord for? How do they feel, having made their own cord much like their prehistoric ancestors would have? Would they like to try to make more another time, using different materials? (Nettle is also fantastic for making cord!)

TRY THIS!
To make the cord thicker and stronger, skip the part where you separate out the strands and twist the thicker fibres together. Making it this way is easier for younger children, too.

MAMMOTH, HUNTER, MOUSE

Imagine our prehistoric ancestors out hunting a six-ton woolly mammoth, with their bows and arrows at the ready. Now imagine those same ancestors being afraid of a tiny mouse! This game pulls together the high energy of spring and the thrill of the chase, in which each character in the game has the ability to catch another. It's full of baffled faces and laughs, and best of all, no players have to leave the game when captured as they simply switch sides!

Requiring team work, this game is a great way to bring a group together. Trying to avoid capture involves running and dodging, building coordination and gross motor skills. Being able to switch sides in the game, rather than being "out", allows any feelings of disappointment they may have to be explored in an encouraging way, developing abilities to self-regulate emotions. Remembering to tag someone lightly can also help to develop empathy. Most of all, this game is enormous fun to watch and play, as children take on the characteristics of each animal and dart about, some invariably forgetting who can chase who. We love this game, as do the children – especially as we are usually the first caught!

LOCATION	Woodland clearings, where trees and animals can set the scene, are ideal, but any outdoor space where children can run will work too
AGE GROUP	4 years +
NUMBER OF PLAYERS	8 +
LEARNING ABOUT ...	Being active ⚙ physical skills ⚙ teamwork ⚙ self-reliance ⚙ self-regulation ⚙ empathy ⚙ confidence ⚙ strategic thinking ⚙ role play ⚙ memory skills
KIT	⇢ 6 cones to mark out the play area ⇢ String to mark the central playing line

Get ready

Place your cones down on the ground to form a rectangle large enough for players to run around in – this will be the pitch or playing area. Now place your string across the middle of the pitch. This will be the half-way line, where the two teams meet at the start of each round. Behind the players at both ends of the playing arena will be each team's "home", which they run to when being chased by the other team. Choose or ask the children to form two teams (preferably even in number and ability).

Get set

Now for the rules of the game. Explain to
the children that each team as a whole can
choose to be one of three characters in the
game as a whole: the hunter, the mammoth, or
the mouse. Hunters can chase the mammoths,
while the mammoths chase the mice. The mice,
in turn, chase the hunters. The action for the hunter
is to pull back on an imaginary bow and arrow. If they
choose to be mammoths, they swing their arm back and forth in
front of their face like a trunk. The sign of the mouse is putting
your hands above your head like ears. As well as these three, there
is also a surprise animal – a dragon, which you become by holding
your hands out in front of you like claws while roaring loudly. The
dragon chases away all the other animals, but can only be used
once by each team, so think carefully about when to use it!

Before the game starts, have the teams decide which of the
characters they will be first, without telling the other team what
they have chosen. Have the teams stand either side of the central
line facing each other. Now tell them to take one big step back.

Go!

When everyone is ready, give the children a countdown – three,
two, one – Go! On "Go!", each team has to mime the character they
have chosen to be. So, one team may have decided to become a
mammoth and will swing their arms back and forth like trunks.
The other team, however, has chosen to be a hunter, and they will
pull back on their imaginary bow and arrows. Seeing this, the

mammoths then quickly turn and run back to their home base, while the hunters pick up the chase and try to tag the mammoths before they reach home! If any mammoths are caught, these players now join the capturing team. If a player makes it home, they stay in their original team. Both sides now come back to the central line for another round of the game.

Three, two, one – Go! The team who were hunters in the first round have chosen to be mice and the other team have chosen to be hunters. This time, the hunters turn to run home, while the mice try to tag them. Again, anyone captured joins the other team.

The game can carry on like this for many turns until all the players are on one side. It's handy to have a few trial runs before the game begins as it can be tricky to remember who chases who! And remember to watch out for that dragon! Roar!!!

Endings

After the game, you might like to discuss the different animals. For example, did they know that woolly mammoths are the ancestors of the African elephant? Can they guess how tall this majestic animal is (3.3 m/11ft), or how much it weighs? (Up to 6,000kg/95st!) Which animal did they prefer to be in the game and why? How did they feel when they were captured, and why? Were there any difficult feelings once they'd been caught, or was it alright since they simply changed sides?

> **TRY THIS!**
> If shy or new to a group, children can always choose to act as the referee, gaining confidence before they choose to join in with the game!

SISTRUM

One sure sign of spring is the birdsong
that fills the air at this time of the year.
Songbirds breed during these longer,
warmer days when there is plenty of food.
This seasonal switch makes male songbirds
become springtime singers, using sound to
stake out territory and attract partners.
Some begin to sing an hour before sunrise,
filling the dawn with music. This activity gets
everyone thinking about the role that sound
plays in nature, and in human life, too.

Music has always played a big part in human existence – it can
make us happy, peaceful, energized and brings us together in a
language we all understand. One very ancient instrument is the
sistrum, a percussion instrument much like a rattle thought to have
originated with the Ancient Egyptians. They have been made from
clay, brass, bronze and wood. In this activity children will make
their own version of this instrument using wood from the forest
floor and decorating it however they choose.

The task of finding the right type of wood connects children
directly to the environment and introduces them to identification
skills, developing language and an understanding of the sensitive
use of resources. Processing the wood for the instrument will
involve tool use, developing fine motor skills and an awareness of
risk management, building confidence and independence. It also

requires focus, perseverance and patience. Being free to design their own instrument makes the children feel that their ideas have value, raising their sense of self-worth. Playing music together as a group develops an understanding of rhythm along with a sense of empathy and community, while dancing and singing always creates a playful mood that is truly contagious!

LOCATION	Woodland is ideal, but if you have collected your kit first, any outdoor space will do
AGE GROUP	4 years +
LEARNING ABOUT ...	Fine motor skills ❀ tool use ❀ safety and risk management ❀ confidence ❀ independence ❀ nature connections ❀ identification skills ❀ language development ❀ sustainability ❀ focus ❀ perseverance ❀ patience ❀ individuality ❀ self-worth ❀ rhythm ❀ empathy ❀ community
KIT	→ Secateurs → Gardening gloves (one pair per person) → Potato peelers (one per person) → Coloured multipurpose pens → Coloured wool or string / → metal bottle caps (3–4 per person) → Small hammer → 1 x 7cm- (2¾in-) long, 3mm-round wire nail, or similar → Thin floristry wire (thinner than nail) → Wire cutters
OPTIONAL	→ Blanket or tarp to sit on, sheath knife or pen knife, tree stump or flat piece of wood

Get ready

Ask the children to hunt on the forest floor for Y-shaped sticks roughly 30cm (12in) long, with the two protruding ends of the "Y" roughly 2cm (¾in) in diameter. Avoid rotten or very dry wood, which is more likely to snap. If enough sticks of the right size and shape are not available on the ground, you might need to take some directly from a nearby common tree (seek permission from the landowner). If so, make a clean cut using secateurs, without tearing the bark, to enable the tree to heal. Capable older children can use secateurs themselves, under supervision (see pages 12–14).

Get set

Now you are ready to create your sistrums. It's fun to all sit on the ground together with the sticks and decorative tools and materials laid out on a tarp or blanket if you have one. Demonstrate how to make a sistrum and allow the children to follow along as you go. First, peel the bark from the stick using a potato peeler, wearing a glove on your helper hand and making sure you always cut away from the body and follow the tool safety rules (see pages 12–14). Placing elbows on knees and working away from the body when peeling the sticks keeps limbs out of harm's way. If some of the bark remains on the stick's nooks and grooves, you can use a knife to clear it away. Younger children will need help here, but older children who seem capable could try the knifework under close adult supervision.

TRY THIS!
Let the children know they don't have to peel the handle if they plan to wrap string around it – especially good if little hands tire easily!

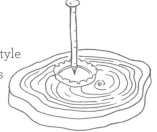

Go!

Now the wood is clean, it can be decorated in any style you like using the coloured pens and/or the lengths of wool or string, perhaps wrapping them around the handle.

Now take your bottle caps – four is a good number – and place them on the ground (it can help to have a hard surface underneath). Using the hammer and the nail, make a hole in the middle of each cap. Take a length of floristry wire long enough to wrap across the Y-shaped end of your stick (see illustration on page 36) and cut this with the wire cutters. Now thread the caps onto the wire (having two back to back makes a good sound!) and tie around the top of your stick, twisting each end to secure. Again, assist younger children while allowing capable older kids to have a go.

Sistrums to the ready, play a tune together! Try playing in time with the birds or choreograph a group dance. You could have a willing lead player whose actions the others in the group have to copy in response. As the game unfolds, it will be full of laughter and antics!

Endings

Look at all the sistrums and admire how unique and different each one is. Would the children like to play their sistrums one by one, to hear each instrument's distinctive sound? You might like to ask them about their favourite song, and whether they would like to try to play it while singing along. Talk about how old this instrument is, dating back to the ancient Egyptians and Greeks who played it in ceremonies and religious festivals.

EARTH DAY BIRTHDAY CAKE

With each birthday we celebrate another year of life and a new beginning. Spring is a season of fresh beginnings when many animals are born and the land is transformed – colourful and vibrant with blossom and flowers, ready for emerging bugs to feast on the nectar and pollinate the fruits to come. We can think of this explosion of life and colour as nature's way of celebrating another year – so what better way to join in than by throwing a birthday party!

Celebrating the Earth is a wonderful way to reconnect all of us to nature and, with a cake at centre stage, what could be more fun? This is messy play at its best: a mud cake made from earth and water, decorated with nature's gems – fallen petals, leaves, sticks and stones . . . whatever the forest floor provides to inspire the designer.

This active free play enables children to become fully immersed in and connected to the environment. As they look for and carry their chosen decorations, noticing the different textures and shapes of the objects they find, their senses are fully engaged, helping them to develop both physically and cognitively, to better understand, interact with and navigate the world around them. Pretending to bake, decorate and eat the cake fires up the imagination and inspires creative thinking. And celebrating the world together in this activity connects us not only to the Earth, but also to each other, developing a sense of community,

empathy and hopefully inspiring a future generation of environmental custodians.

Get ready

This is definitely an activity for old clothes that no one will mind getting dirty. Choose a spot for your celebrations – somewhere with lots of soil. Make sure it is free of litter, and near to fallen petals and other natural objects (such as sticks, pebbles and feathers) to use to decorate the cake. Choose a spot of soil within this area that will be the cake-making station. Ask the children to collect water (from a natural source, if there is one) in the

LOCATION	Any natural area with soil and trees	
AGE GROUP	2 years +	
LEARNING ABOUT ...	Being active ⊕ teamwork ⊕ community ⊕ empathy ⊕ role play ⊕ sensory experiences ⊕ nature connections ⊕ imagination ⊕ creativity ⊕ sustainability	
KIT	→ Water (if a nearby source is not available) → Containers to carry	water (suitable for little hands) → Trowels/small spades (for everyone)
OPTIONAL	→ Buckets, wooden spoons, cupcake cases, paper plates, candles (wax or flameless) and a lighter/matches, rubbish bags, hand-washing kit	

containers and transport it to the cake-making station. If you are not using spoons, they can also collect some sticks for mixing the "cake mixture".

Get set

Trowels in hand, everyone who wants to can now help dig a hole. If you live in an area of clay soil, mud can easily be made in the ground by pouring water into the hole and then adding the loose soil back in. If the soil is more sandy and water is likely to seep away, put the soil and water into a bucket or similar container. Mix well using sticks or spoons. Make as little or as much as you like.

Go!

Once they've made the mud, it's time for the children to build the cake! Using the trowels or bare hands, they can start piling up the mud in the chosen spot, moulding the cake into whatever shape they like – a rectangle, round or all misshapen . . . anything goes! Once they've got a shape they like, they can start to add some natural decorations. As this is a cake for the Earth, ask the children to find decorations they think the Earth would like. They can explore their surroundings as they search for the perfect feather, stick, pebble or fallen petal. You could also make other party food, such as mud sausages or mud marshmallows on a stick or mud cupcakes (if you have brought cases).

Once the cake is complete, it's time to add your candles (these can be candles that you've brought, or pretend wooden stick ones). Gather everyone together to sing "Happy Birthday" to the Earth. Maybe the children will want to pretend to eat the cake or leave it for the Earth and its creatures. Celebrations may continue with party games, or it may feel like the right time to end. Before leaving, have everyone gather up any litter to take home.

TRY THIS!
If the children are reluctant to touch mud, reassure them that they can always wash their hands. If necessary, mold the mud for them and before long they'll be joining in too!

Endings

At the end of the activity, you might like to discuss with the children what the Earth might like as a gift on its birthday. Some ideas could include planting a new tree, putting up a bird feeder, or using less water. This can open up great discussions about how we can all be more friendly to the environment. We are a part of the world, so when we look after it, we are looking after ourselves, too. You could ask the children how old everyone thinks the Earth is (4,543 billion years!), and how long people have lived on it (in humankind's modern form, about 200,000 years). You may like to talk about what the children love best about our planet. Let the conversation take its own course – we find that, it usually ends up somewhere amazing.

SPRING DAY OUT

Here is a plan for a day out full of springtime activities, each inspired by the spirit of renewal that permeates this time of year. The vernal equinox (which takes place each year between 20–23 March in the northern hemisphere and between 20–23 September in the southern hemisphere) marks the first day of astronomical spring and is the moment when day is the same length as night. From now on, the days will continue to grow longer until the summer solstice.

Spring is also the season for Easter celebrations, which in the northern hemisphere falls on the first Sunday following the full moon and the vernal equinox. For Christians, the Easter egg is a symbol of the resurrection. Eggs, however, as symbols of creation and new life, have been associated with spring rebirth and creation celebrations for millennia. The Ancient Egyptians believed that the sun god Ra hatched from a primal egg. The idea of a cosmic egg that gave birth the universe is found in many cultures, civilizations and religions. Whatever your beliefs, the sharing of eggs (especially decorated and chocolate ones!) is a joyful experience. To tie in with the spring celebrations, we've chosen an egg hunt as the first activity.

The second activity draws inspiration from the hare, which is traditionally associated with spring. You might have heard the expression "mad as a March hare" – a saying that refers to the sight of hares leaping in the air and boxing each other. These matches

LOCATION	A woodland clearing is ideal
AGE GROUP	3 years +
LEARNING ABOUT ...	Health ✿ community ✿ achievement ✿ self-esteem ✿ sharing ✿ empathy ✿ focus ✿ nature connections ✿ plant identification ✿ sustainability ✿ stewardship ✿ independence ✿ self-reliance ✿ fine motor skills ✿ creativity ✿ observation ✿ imagination ✿ transferable skills and ideas ✿ learning and memories ✿ history ✿ culture ✿ freedom and space
FLOW OF THE DAY	This order of activities has worked for us on our Forest School days, but please take hints from your own group on how to set out your day and feel free to change the sequence if needed. Also, factor in a lunch break when the time is right.

take place in March during their breeding season. The fact that this activity takes place during the rebirth of the land in spring has lead to hares being used as symbols of fertility since ancient times and of course hares (or, now more commonly, rabbits) are connected to Easter. With this in mind, it seems fitting to feature the hare in our spring day out, which we do by making clay artworks of this spirited animal.

To round off the day, we take advantage of the flowers of the season and forage for dandelions (*Tarazacum officinale*) to make a delicious springtime tea.

Darting around together being active is of course part of the egg hunt, allowing excited energy to be used and developing a sense of team work all while having fun. Discovering the hidden treasure fills everyone with feelings of achievement, raising self-esteem. Sharing food, whether it be chocolate eggs or a cup of tea, provides a space for empathy to be explored and strengthens a group's connection. Learning to gather and taste wild food brings children closer to the environment, focusing their minds and allowing plant-identification skills to be developed. Thinking sustainably about our use of wild foods furthers our connection to the natural world and engenders a sense of stewardship in each child, while knowing that food can always be found enhances feelings of independence and self-reliance.

Using natural materials to make unique pieces of art develops the children's observation and fine motor skills, stimulates creativity and allows natural objects to be seen in new and exciting ways. As a piece of art, these ideas, experiences and memories can then be taken home, to open up conversations and encourage the further sharing of knowledge, deepening the learning experience. It's interesting, for example, to look into what people believed in the past about different animals and plants to broaden understanding of the natural world, as well as of the ancient practices that underlie some of what we still do and believe today. Running around on a spring day fills our lungs with fresh air and our emotions with happiness and a sense of freedom. Enjoy!

Activity 1: THE EGG HUNT

Get ready

Choose an area to spend your day in, making sure that it is suitable
for all the activities you plan to do (for example, if you'd like to
make dandelion tea, pick a spot where these flowers are growing
nearby). Making sure the children don't see what you're doing,
hide your golden tickets in this area – in the knots of trees, under
bushes or anywhere you like, just remember to keep in mind how
many there are and where you've hidden them! While this is taking
place, the children could explore the area a little or gather in a
talking circle with another adult present. You could have a chat

KIT	→ Golden tickets (or any colour of your choice, making sure you have three times as many as your group's number)
	→ Chocolate Easter eggs (enough for your group)
OPTIONAL	→ Alternative eggs (such as dairy free) if needed to accommodate allergies, blanket for sitting on

about eggs and the species that lay them, like birds, lizards, snakes, and tortoises, whose young all hatch from eggs. Talk about how birds may make a nest for their eggs to keep them safe, asking the children what materials they use for this (sticks, mud, feathers and so on).

Get set

Now let the children know that they will be going on an egg hunt with a difference! The key to getting their chocolate eggs will be finding the tickets hidden in the surrounding area. What's more, just like birds build a shelter to protect their eggs, so the group will first have to build a giant nest to house any golden tickets they find. Explain that it doesn't matter how many golden tickets each person finds – they need to work as a team to find them all, and everyone will get a chocolate egg once all the tickets have been discovered.

Once everyone is ready, ask the children to find as many sticks as they can in order to build the special nest, collecting them together in a big pile. Let them decide how elaborate the nest should be. Maybe they will want to weave their sticks together to form a circle, or simply place them on top of each other. They might want to lay down sticks to make a base or just leave it as bare ground. Do they want to decorate the nest? You can have a lot of fun playing around with this.

Go!

When everyone agrees that the nest is finished, point out the area in which the tickets are hidden, and start the hunt! Let the children know that, once they find a ticket, they should bring it straight back to the nest. (Adults will want to keep count, as the query "How many are left?" will be repeatedly asked by the children!) Once all the tickets are found, bring out the chocolate eggs and share them out equally. Enjoy the celebration.

Endings

While everyone is sitting down enjoying their chocolate eggs, take the opportunity to start a discussion with the children about the significance of eggs, spring and Easter, pointing out, for example, that many of the things we do today originate in ancient pagan celebrations. Do they know that Easter eggs used to be dyed duck eggs and that chocolate eggs as we know them today didn't arrive until the 19th century?

Ask about their hunt – did they find it hard or did it help knowing that they were searching as a team? How easy or difficult was it to make the nest, and would they do anything differently if they were to make another one? Do they now have a new appreciation for how skilful birds must be?

With lots of energy expended and the group feeling more connected as a team, now is a good time to offer a more focused activity.

Activity 2: CLAY ART

Get ready

First demonstrate how to make clay art. Have some natural decorations (such as fallen petals or pebbles, leaves and feathers) to hand; the children will hunt for their own later. If you don't have toothpicks, you will need a stick that is sharp enough to puncture paper with small dot holes. If it's too blunt, sharpen the end with a knife. Press out the clay between your hands to make a rectangle the size of your piece of cardboard, keeping it roughly 2–3cm (1in) thick. Leave the clay on top of the cardboard and put them both to one side.

Next, draw an outline of a hare on a piece of paper (you could use the one *below* as a guide), remembering not to make it larger than your piece of clay. Don't worry, it doesn't have to be perfect! Just the general shape of a hare will do. Lay the paper on top of the clay and press down to secure. Take your stick or toothpick and make small holes through the paper along the outline of your drawing, quite close together. Once complete, remove the paper – you should see the exact copy of your dot drawing on the clay. Add your decorations by pressing them carefully into the clay, before adding your initials to complete your art. Leave to dry, ideally in the sun. Once dry, the cardboard can be removed.

KIT	→ Penknife or equivalent
	→ Clay, enough for everyone to have a flattened rectangle piece approx 15 x 12cm (6 x 4in) in size and 2–3cm (1in) thick
	→ Pieces of cardboard of equivalent size (one per person)
	→ Paper, pencils and rubbers for group
	→ A box and bag to carry the clay art home
	→ Rubbish bags
OPTIONAL	→ Blanket, tarps (for shelter and seating), toothpicks, hare template (to fit size of the clay), scissors, tracing paper, craft beads

Get set

Demo over, it's time for the children to go off to forage for their decorations. Ask them to choose from what the forest floor provides, leaving any spring flowers to flourish and grow. If you haven't brought toothpicks, everyone also needs to look for a small stick to draw with.

Go!

As the team returns, hand out all the materials needed for their art. The theme for this activity is hares, but everyone can choose their own design if they wish to. If the sticks are too blunt, you may want to sharpen them for little ones, while capable older kids can try this for themselves under supervision (see pages 12–14). In a large group, make sure that all clay pieces have the artists' initials on them so that they can be easily identified after they have been made and set to one side to dry, ready to be taken home.

TRY THIS!
If you have clay soil in your area, this can be used, though you will need tools to dig it out. It can crack and shrink when drying, so permanence is not a guarantee!

Endings

Take an interest in each piece of art, talking through what inspired it with the artist and what they like about it. Every time we have done this activity, we have been amazed at how wonderful these pieces are, all in their own unique way.

You might like to discuss the properties of clay. For example, have they noticed how clay soil shrinks or swells as it dries out in the sun or is soaked by the rain. How does it feel when it's wet? When it's heated to high temperatures it becomes a rock-like substance called ceramic, used in pottery to make all sorts of things like plates, pots and cups. Would the children like to try pottery in the future?

Can they think of a famous hare? How about the March Hare from *Alice's Adventures in Wonderland*? Lewis Caroll was inspired to create him after witnessing hares boxing.

With minds focused and energy now levelling out, it's a good time to return their attention to the environment by foraging for food that can be enjoyed as a group.

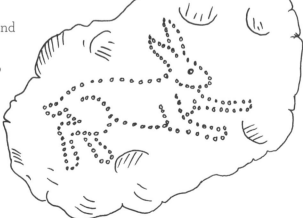

Activity 3: DANDELION AND LIME TEA

Get ready

Before letting the children go off to forage for dandelions, show one to the group, with its very distinctive bright yellow petals and toothed leaves, so everyone knows what they should be looking for. Give each forager a cup, and head out to where the dandelions are growing. Once they've positively identified them, show the group how to pick only the flowerhead by pinching it off the stalk, then pop it in your cup. Let the children know not to worry if some stalks are gathered – all parts of this plant are edible, but the yellow

KIT	→ Cups (2 per person)
	→ Cold water, enough to cool drinks, wash hands and flowers
	→ Limes (enough for half a lime per person)
	→ Sharp knife
	→ Runny honey
	→ Thermos of hot water, enough for group
OPTIONAL	→ Tea strainer, teaspoon, sugar, picnic or packed lunches for all

flowers are the sweetest part and its stalks and leaves are more bitter. Now let the children gather flowers to put in their own cup – they only need a handful each. Help younger children identify the correct plant.

Get set

Once enough flowers have been collected, gather the group back at your base camp area. Check that everyone only has dandelions in their cups and pour cold water into each to gently wash the flowers – and help any bugs that may be present to escape! Some children will like to inspect any bugs that may emerge, but reassure and help those that may be nervous. After a good swill, place your hands over the top of the cup to act as a strainer and tip away the water, or use a tea strainer, if you have one. Adults should then halve the limes and hand out one half to each maker (for some a quarter may be enough).

Go!

Hand out fresh cups (if needed) and have the children place their washed dandelions into it. Ask everyone to squeeze the lime juice into their cup and then add about a teaspoon of honey (you can use sugar if you prefer). Ask everyone to place their cups on the floor and pour in hot water. Let older children do this if they want and assist younger ones to avoid any possible scalds. Leave to steep for 5–10 mins, after which the water should have a slight yellow tinge. Add cold water now if it's still too hot to sip. It's now ready to drink – sit back and enjoy this refreshing wild tea with the rest of the group.

> **TRY THIS!**
> If you cannot find dandelion flowerheads, a quarter cup of their leaves can be used to make tea instead.

Endings

As everyone is enjoying their tea, ask the children what they think of it. Would they have it again? Would they add anything different?

You might like to talk about how useful the dandelion is – from its roots to its flower tips. As well as being used in teas like the one they've just made, its leaves can be eaten in salads, and soft yellow dyes can be extracted from its petals. It can also be used as a medicine. The health benefits of dandelions are many – this plant is full of vitamins and minerals, as well as being rich in fibre and an antioxidant. It can help cleanse the body and treat skin infections.

Dandelions are sun lovers, they open their flowers to greet the morning sun and close them again in the evening. Some people think of the dandelion as a representation of three celestial bodies: the sun (the yellow flower); the moon (the puff ball of seeds); and the stars (the seeds once they've been blown into the air) . . . A truly amazing plant.

Summer

The days grow longer and warmer, while the high, renewing energy of spring is settling down to a steadier pace: summer has arrived.

Nature's more relaxed energy seems to transfer over onto us humans, too. Our pace slows and our muscles relax – lying back on the soft grass seems the natural thing to do.

At our own Forest School, we have noticed how the warmer weather means children are comfortable settling down outside and really focusing on an intricate activity where fingers are not restricted by the cold.

We have seen how with lighter summer clothes and nature bursting with colour and life, there is no need to be in any particular location, as the children's attention is drawn to what's around them. In fact, often the simple act of walking becomes an activity in itself, with many discoveries popping up along the way for the groups to share, whether it be a jewel beetle glistening in the sun, speckled wood butterflies fighting for their territory, or the sweet scent of lime tree flowers – a feast for the senses.

Enjoy these wonderful summertime activities and all that glorious nature in bloom has to offer.

BARK MASKS

Mask making has roots in so many cultures across the globe, from the ritual masks created by African or Amazonian tribes that incorporate bark cloth, to modern masks used in contemporary art and dance. Ancient or modern, these masks can disguise the wearer and transform them into a mythical creature, an animal, a tree . . . the options are as wide as the maker's imagination.

Wearing masks made from natural materials is a great way to celebrate the summer season, allowing the maker to become part of the surrounding landscape. The trees and plants of summer have put in immense energy to power their growth and create the flowers and seeds of the next generation. With this in mind, bark that has been shed by trees provides the ideal material to make masks during this season, as it causes no damage; if leaves or flowers were used, busy plants would have to divert essential energy into repair.

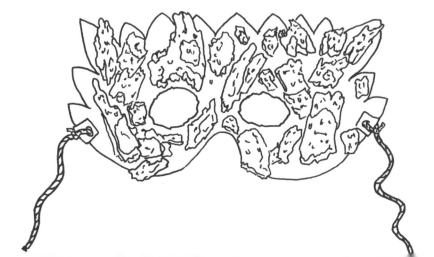

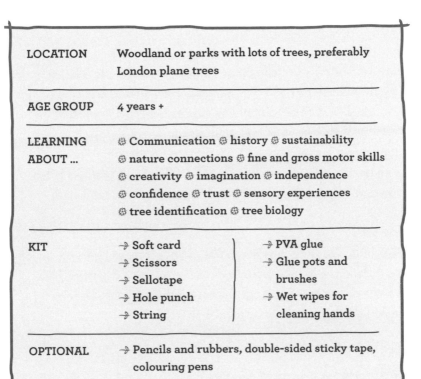

LOCATION	Woodland or parks with lots of trees, preferably London plane trees
AGE GROUP	4 years +
LEARNING ABOUT ...	✿ Communication ✿ history ✿ sustainability ✿ nature connections ✿ fine and gross motor skills ✿ creativity ✿ imagination ✿ independence ✿ confidence ✿ trust ✿ sensory experiences ✿ tree identification ✿ tree biology
KIT	⇥ Soft card ⇥ Scissors ⇥ Sellotape ⇥ Hole punch ⇥ String ⇥ PVA glue ⇥ Glue pots and brushes ⇥ Wet wipes for cleaning hands
OPTIONAL	⇥ Pencils and rubbers, double-sided sticky tape, colouring pens

This activity opens up opportunities for conversations about ancient human history and traditional practices that still take place today. Finding the right trees and bark enhances the children's knowledge of trees. As well as a sensory experience, gathering the materials and creating the masks is a great way of developing a child's gross and fine motor skills. This is a truly creative activity, in which the children are free to shape their own piece of work, unconstrained by any defined outcome, which boosts their sense of independence and confidence. Sharing the finished piece develops trust and group connections and opens up a world of imagination.

Get ready

Show everyone a London plane tree (*Platanus x acerifolia*), a large deciduous tree with shiny green maple-like leaves and camouflage-patterned bark of olive, grey and cream. Let them know that the outer bark is the tree's protection: a non-living layer that covers the living layer just underneath it. Any harm to this living layer could damage the tree, so they should only collect bark that has fallen onto the ground. They will be making masks out of this bark.

Get set

Ask all makers to gather a handful of bark from the ground, looking for different colours, shapes and sizes that catch their eye. Bark collected, you can all set out the rest of the materials needed for making the masks and settle down to get creative.

Go!

Now the mask makers should take a piece of card large enough to cover the top half of their face and cut it into any shape they want. Don't forget the eye holes. To make sure these are in the right place, each maker can line the card up against their face and feel where one of their eyes is, then move the card away from their face while holding this point with their fingers until they can safely cut it away. Then they can fold the card lightly in two in order to cut the second eye slot that mirrors and lines up with the first. If they are slightly out of shape, they can always tweak and cut away what's needed. They can also cut a gap for their nose, if needed.

The places where string will be attached on either side of the mask can be strengthened by sticking on a strip of tape (roughly level with where the ears will be). Use a hole punch to punch through the card and tape on both sides. Take two pieces of string and tie one on each side of the mask, making sure they are long enough to tie the mask at the back of the head. Now the mask makers can break their bark into pieces (small pieces tend to stick better). Get them to apply glue to the card and then stick on the bark. Young children may find glue a bit tricky; if so, double-sided sticky tape works well.

Everyone will have their own approach to making their masks. Our son decided that the string holes should go further in from the edge, so the card fanned out once tied. It looked amazing! Some may want to use felt tips to add decoration, or create a design in pencil before colouring it in. Once the masks are done, it's time to transform . . . we have had many masked performances in our Forest School sessions, featuring fairies, insects, warriors and even aliens!

Endings

Invite the makers to talk about their masks: what do they become once the mask is on and why did they choose this? How do they feel wearing their masks? You could discuss how people have used masks for many years in ceremonies and rituals. In African culture, for example, masks are used in wedding ceremonies and other rites of passage. How old do they think the oldest mask is? The oldest known mask, made of stone, dates back some 9,000 years!

TRY THIS!
If you do not have access to a London plane tree, many others shed bark, including birch, shagbark hickory, Scots pine and eucalyptus.

BLACKBERRY INK AND FEATHER QUILL PENS

Blackberries are abundant on bramble bushes in mid-summer, when the fruits are plump, purple-black and juicy. Our Forest School groups love to use this remarkable plant for all sorts of activities – this one involves making ink to use with a quill pen.

Lots of different natural materials have been used over the centuries to make ink, including soil minerals (such as graphite) and charcoal, as well as plant roots, nuts and berries. In fact, berries – readily available through the summer months – were often used to make ink by soldiers in the American Civil War, when other sources became too expensive or unobtainable.

Our local park is home to many wetland birds, including Canada geese which are easily recognizable with their black heads and necks, bright white cheeks and rumps, and brown bodies. Each summer their gorgeous wing feathers moult, leaving our Forest School groups spoilt for choice when making quill pens. The children dart about gathering handfuls of feathers, eagerly waving them in the air shouting: "I've found another one!" We like to leave a treat for our birds as a little thank you, and so bring handfuls of lettuce and cabbage. The whole activity makes for real, good old-fashioned fun on a summer's day.

LOCATION	Woodland and parks with ponds or lakes are ideal
AGE GROUP	6 years +
LEARNING ABOUT...	Identification skills ❀ natural seasonal rhythms ❀ sustainability ❀ nature connections ❀ patience ❀ creativity ❀ imagination ❀ gross and fine motor skills ❀ risk assessment and management ❀ independence ❀ confidence ❀ focus ❀ empathy ❀ communication ❀ trust
KIT	→ Cup-size collection pots (one per person) → Teaspoons → White vinegar → Table salt → Scissors → Paper
OPTIONAL	→ Water, feathers (one per person) if not available locally, tea strainer/sieve, clean, cup-size pot; fine-grain sandpaper, small pot with lid (for ink)

This activity helps children learn how to identify useful wild materials, as well as what is available when, creating nature connections and gaining an understanding of their sustainable use. Seeing that natural resources can have multiple uses encourages creative thinking. This activity gets children running around collecting items, then practising their fine motor skills as they transform these into the tools they need. Creating ink artworks takes imagination, confidence and patience, and sharing the pieces allows the group to explore feelings of empathy, trust and communication. A wonderfully creative summertime activity.

Get ready

Set off on the search for blackberries and feathers, having fun while gathering all you need. If you think finding both feathers and berries on the same site will be difficult, you can always bring some feathers along with you. When gathering blackberries, bear in mind that each maker will need roughly half a cup of berries to make a small well of ink. If anyone wants to eat blackberries, which is highly likely, it's not a bad idea to have some water to wash them. If you feel they need guiding, have them show you what they want to eat before they eat it! It's worth reminding them that some berries are poisonous. Each maker also needs to find a blunt-ended stick. This will be their pestle for pounding the blackberries.

Get set

Once gathered, find a nice spot to sit down and pound the blackberries in the cups to extract the juice. If makers wish to remove any bits they can pour the juice through a tea strainer or sieve and into a clean pot. Each person then adds half a teaspoon of vinegar and half a teaspoon of salt, mixing together. Ink done, now on to the quills!

Let everyone choose a feather. To make the pen nib, cut the the rounded tip of the feather away at a 45-degree angle with a pair of scissors. Then, cut across the very end of the point so that there are a few millimetres of flat edge to write with. Now cut a small slit down the middle of this newly made end. This creates a fairly

TRY THIS!
Try out different feathers for the quills – turkey feathers work well too!

rustic version of a quill tip, but it works well to write with. Let younger children have a go but feathers can be surprisingly tough, so assist with the cutting if needed. Older kids may also wish to clear some of the lower feathers from their quills to give their hands more gripping space. To do this, they can cut away the feathers and sand down the shaft to make it smooth.

Go!

Now comes the exciting bit! The children can dip their quills into their ink and use it on the paper. Do they want to write their name, draw a picture or a pattern, leave a message for their friends or even write a story? Let them know that the ink will first appear purple/red but with time will turn black on the paper. It will not smudge either – in all, a fantastic natural ink! Some may wish to take their ink home – a small container with a lid is handy for this.

Endings

Invite the children to share what they have made with everyone else. Had they imagined before that blackberries could be used as ink? Ask them what other natural ingredients they think would make good ink. Perhaps other berries, like elderberries, raspberries and strawberries? You could also ask what writing with a feather felt like. In the Western world, quill pens were the main writing tools used from the 6th right up until the 19th century, when metal pens were invented and mass produced. Even today, white quills are placed on counsel tables each day the court sits in the US Supreme Court – testimony to this amazing natural tool's usefulness and value!

INTUITION

It's summer: life is in full flow and the birds and animals born earlier in the year are being taught all that's needed to survive. Parents of all sorts of species are on full alert, trying to make sure that nothing happens to their precious babies. To do this, they use every sense they have to stay safe: sight, hearing, smell . . . and intuition – that sense of "just knowing". Humans have this sense, too. You know the feeling that makes you suddenly turn and look in the opposite direction, only to see that someone is looking at you or trying to get your attention from afar? That's intuition!

This game taps into this subtle sense. When we have played it at our Forest School sessions, the children are always amazed and stunned at how precise this "knowing" can be (as are we!). A sense of awe ripples through the group and hands dart up in eager anticipation to be the next to play. As it involves having to sit still and quiet, tuning into what is being played out all around you, this is a wonderful game to play on a warm summer's day when your mind can be still and your muscles can relax.

This game requires a calm mental state, sometimes called "mindfulness", which is achieved by gently focusing your attention on the present moment, acknowledging any thoughts or feelings you have but not holding onto or acting upon them – a valuable tool often overlooked in our busy modern lives. The game also requires empathy toward the other players as children patiently wait for their turn and understand that any disruption will negatively affect the game and the other players. This deepens a sense of trust and teamwork within the group. It also allows the player who is sensing what they feel to develop trust in their own feelings, which in turn deepens their confidence. This game provides an opportunity to be completely immersed in the moment, listening to the sounds of the birds and insects, feeling a summer's breeze, smelling the plants and soil. It's a great way of connecting with nature and discovering a skill that is shared by both humans and animals. Prepare to be amazed!

LOCATION	Any natural outdoor location will do, but woodland areas with lots of creatures, sounds and smells make ideal spots
AGE GROUP	4 years +
NUMBER OF PLAYERS	6 +
LEARNING ABOUT ...	Instinct ✿ patience ✿ focus ✿ teamwork ✿ being calm ✿ mindfulness ✿ animal behaviour ✿ nature connections ✿ empathy ✿ trust ✿ confidence
KIT	⇢ Blindfold

Get ready

Gather everyone round and have them sit in a circle. To set the scene, talk about the gut instinct or intuition that we all have. Ask whether anyone has any stories to tell of experiencing this or if they have seen pets or wild animals display it.

Get set

Run through the rules of the game before you start so everyone knows what will happen, explaining that it will only work if everyone in the circle is very quiet and focused. Select the player who will be trying out their intuition first (the "middle player"), quelling any disappointment at this point by letting everyone know that they will have a turn at being the middle player, if they wish. The middle player sits down in the middle of the circle made by the other players and puts on a blindfold. Once everyone is in place, select another player from the surrounding circle (the "circle player"), without the middle player knowing who or where this person is.

Explain that when the game begins, the circle player will stare with happy, focused intent on the middle player, perhaps silently calling their name or saying hello in their mind, while everyone else bows their head, shuts their eyes and stills their thoughts. To help them quiet their minds, players can listen to all the summer woodland sounds around them. When the middle player feels they have sensed the focus on them, they will point in the direction that they feel the stare coming from. They don't have to pinpoint the precise direction, just the general area. You will all be surprised at how often this direction is found and even pinpointed.

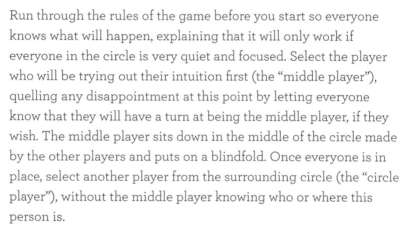

Go!

Remind everyone that the game will only work if they are very quiet and still their thoughts. When everyone is ready, let the game begin – it will end with lots of gasps and giggles as the middle player points toward the circle player! Once all the excitement has passed, play another round, until all the children have had a go in the roles of middle and circle players. Amazing intuition!

Endings

Ask how it felt to be stared at as the middle player – what was it that made them point toward where they thought the stare was coming from? When they were the person staring, did they think anything in any particular (such as words) to will the middle player on? How did it feel to be still and quiet? Did they notice any sounds or smells when they were sitting with their eyes closed? Did they feel the wind or hear the leaves rustle? Ask why they think animals might want stay alert, and how this could help them survive.

TRY THIS!
To keep player selection random, you could have everyone stand in a circle, close your eyes and spin in the middle of them with your finger pointing out, stopping after a couple of turns. Where your finger points, that's the middle player. Repeat for the circle player.

NATURE WATCH

In some Native American tribes, it is said, hunters would go out alone to a favoured spot in the wild and sit quietly. If a hunter's arrival disrupted the wildlife around him, he would wait, remaining perfectly still, until the natural tranquillity returned. Here in the forest or on the grassland he would sit, quieten his mind and become watchful, learning more about the place around him – becoming part of it.

For most of us, the days when we had to hunt for our food have long passed. We tend to visit wild places rather than live within them. When we go to a natural place, especially as part of a group, it's easy to amble along talking and laughing and forget to look up at the beauty around us and check in with the feelings this evokes. This activity provides the opportunity to be still, to become aware of what's around us, and to tune into how we feel in this watchful mood.

When we are calm and quiet within a natural space, wildlife will often come closer to us. We sense the ground beneath us, feel the wind brush against our skin and pick up scents in the air. We become part of the living landscape again.

This game requires the players to be in a quiet, still and observant mood, so it works well after lunch on a warm summer's day or after energy has been spent in a more active game or hike. It can be just what's needed after a hectic and loud week at school (or, for the adults, work!), where space and stillness are rare commodities.

This structured activity focuses the mind and provides opportunities to develop patience, while sharing these personal experiences deepens trust and empathy, and brings groups closer together. It allows children to explore their feelings and an emotional language to be used, developing communication and self-awareness.

LOCATION	Woodland with its diverse landscapes is great, but other wild spaces work too
AGE GROUP	5 years +
LEARNING ABOUT ...	⊛ Focus ⊛ patience ⊛ nature connections ⊛ trust ⊛ empathy ⊛ teamwork ⊛ self-awareness ⊛ communication
KIT	→ None needed

We are always deeply touched by the responses this activity gives rise to and cherish these special times with our Forest School groups.

Get ready

Take a quiet stroll to your chosen natural place. Set the scene: talk about how Native American hunters would use this technique to learn more about the natural world around them – the world they depended on for survival; the world we still depend on. Explain that it may feel difficult to be still and to quieten our thoughts, but the more we practise, the easier it will become. Encourage them to stick with it and give it a chance.

Get set

Allow the players to find their spot, letting their intuition guide them to their chosen place. Once there, ask them to sit as motionless as they can. For the first few minutes, they should aim to let the world around them settle again, until it is going on as if they were not there. If it helps, they can shut their eyes to begin with. When they are ready, they can open their eyes again and remain perfectly still to observe the scene around them: the birds that pass by, the sound of buzzing insects, the smell of the trees, the leaves that sway in the breeze. At the same time, they can notice how they themselves feel.

Go!

Start your silent watching.

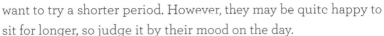

It's useful to set a loose timeframe for
this activity: older children can start with
5-7 minutes, while younger ones may
want to try a shorter period. However, they may be quite happy to
sit for longer, so judge it by their mood on the day.

When the time has come to move back into the group, invite them
to share their experience. Some children (and this has been the case
with us) may want to build something using natural materials as an
expression of their experience, perhaps leaving it as a gift in their
special spot. Allow for whatever comes naturally to the players to
be expressed.

Endings

To help discussions along, ask if there was a plant or an animal that
caught their attention – how did that make them feel? Perhaps they
noticed a colour that they liked or a beetle crawling across the floor.
Did they find it difficult to be still? Or did they
find it relaxing? Did the wildlife seem less
startled by them when they were calm?
Why did they choose their particular
spot? Did they feel comfortable, as if
they belonged there? Would they like
to try it again now, or some time later?

TRY THIS!
For true sharing to
occur, make sure to keep
the tone sensitive and
respectful throughout
any discussions.

SYCAMORE LAUNCHERS

In the summer months, we have great fun in the parks and woods that are home to sycamore trees (*Acer pseudoplatanus*, known as sycamore maples in the US). Their winged seeds are ripening during this season, and will fall to the ground in autumn, twirling like helicopter propellers through the air as they go. This is a chance for the tree's seed to be carried by the wind to an ideal spot where a new generation can grow. For the children at Forest School, this activity is a chance to get up close to these wonderful paired seeds. As they collect spring's ungerminated seeds from the forest floor, the children notice their V-shaped wings. Then, throwing them into the air, excited eyes watch how they glide and twist in their descent before landing back on earth. It's contagious fun!

Making a sycamore launcher shows the children how the seeds achieve their helicopter-like movement. At the start of this activity, they handle, study and play with the delicate seeds, but the aim is to replicate the seeds rather than use them as launchers, as the real seeds might not survive the ride! It's also important to stress that the seeds provide food for mice, slugs and voles and any survivors may yet germinate to produce future generations of trees. For these reasons, to lessen the temptation of collecting fresh seeds, we tend to do this activity in summer, when this year's seeds are still on the trees. This then gets them jumping with joy in autumn when the new seeds start falling!

Creating something that mimics a particular species' natural process helps children to get to know that species, including how to spot it and learn what it does at different times of year. This activity offers a great workout for the kids, as they run around to find the materials needed and collect launched "seeds". Making the launchers themselves develops fine motor skills and brings in elements of maths in a fun, visual way, as well as requiring patience, focus and perseverance, all boosting self-belief, self-regulation and self-reliance. Playing with the launchers brings groups closer together: a successful launch is full of laughs, with faces turned to the sky, minds flying away with their helicopter seeds.

LOCATION	Woodland or parkland with sycamore trees	
AGE GROUP	6 years +	
LEARNING ABOUT...	⊕ Tree identification ⊕ nature connections ⊕ gross and fine motor skills ⊕ mathematics ⊕ patience ⊕ focus ⊕ perseverance ⊕ self-belief ⊕ self-regulation ⊕ self-reliance ⊕ teamwork ⊕ communication ⊕ imagination	
KIT	→ Secateurs → Scissors → Stiff card → Sheath knife	→ Gardening gloves → Double-sided sticky tape → Rubber bands
OPTIONAL	→ Potato peelers, pen	

Get ready

Take a look at some sycamore seeds. You can find last year's offerings beneath the parent tree or you might see some of this year's whirling down early to the ground. Notice how the V-shaped seed is actually two seeds paired together, each with one wing placed at a right angle to the other. When shed, the wind catches these wings and rotates them, slowing their descent and allowing them to disperse from the parent tree. Let everyone play for a while with some seeds to explore how they move. Tell everyone that they will be making their own sycamore seeds to launch.

Get set

Everyone needs to find two strong dry sticks, one for the seed and one for the launcher. The stick for the seed should be roughly 7cm (2¾in) long and about the width of a little finger (smaller flies better). The stick for the launcher should be larger – 12cm (4½in) long and the thickness of a thumb. If necessary, use secateurs to cut the sticks to length (see pages 12–14 for tool safety instructions).

To prepare the sycamore wings for the launcher, each child needs to cut two strips of card roughly 7cm (2¾in) long and 1.5cm (¾in) wide. Set these to one side.

Before carving the sticks, demonstrate the safe working practices for carving using a sheath knife (see pages 12–14). For younger children or those that you feel need more time to understand the safety aspects, you could demonstrate how to use a potato peeler on the tip of the seed stick, and then carve the rest for them yourself. Let those who are capable carve the sticks themselves, keeping careful watch and offering help if necessary. Remind the group that when carving they must stay focused on the job at hand.

Go!

Let the children work along with you, following each step as you go. Holding the smaller stick for the seed in a gloved hand, and cutting away from the body, gently shave off some wood from the tip on one side. Turn the stick around and do the same to the other side, so that you have a flat, clean surface of about 2.5cm (1in) on either side of the stick. At the other end of the seed stick, cut a small 90 degree-shaped notch (as shown in the illustration, left). This will be where the rubber band attaches for launching.

Now, in the longer launcher stick, demonstrate how to cut two V-shaped notches from either side of the stick, which will be where a rubber band is attached (see illustration, below left).

To attach the wings, cut some double-sided sticky tape and place on the carved sections of the seed stick. Place one card wing on the tape, pointing upward in line with the stick, then fold it over just above where it attaches to the stick. This fold line needs to be at a 45-degree angle, which will allow the card wing to jut out at a 90-degree angle to the stick (see illustration, page 78). Do the same on the other side, making sure to fold the card in the opposite direction to the first. That's the seed done!

Now take the launching stick and wrap a rubber band around the notches. Push one end of the band through the other and pull tight – this will help it stay in place (see illustration, page 78).

Once complete, it's time to launch! Wrap the free end of the rubber band around the 90-degree shaped notch on the seed stick. With the launching stick held out in front and up toward the sky, pull back and down on the seed head and ... fire!

Let the kids decide if they want to launch alone or, if in a group, take turns watching each other to see which technique launches the furthest. If anyone struggles, help them work out the best way to set their seeds flying. Amazing twirling fun!

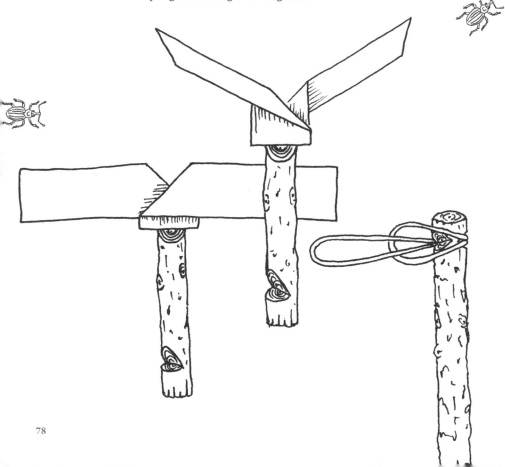

Endings

You can ask how it felt to launch the seeds – would the children change anything about the design or their launching technique? You might like to talk more about the sycamore species and how its free-hanging, yellow-green, late-spring flowers produce lots of nectar. Insects love this sweet sugary substance and readily visit the trees to drink it. This helps to pollinate the flowers (transferring the male pollen grains to the female pollen receptor, called the stigma) that will then go on to make the seeds. Sycamores produce hundreds of seeds – when do the children think the seeds will fall from the tree? (In autumn.) And when do the seeds begin to grow into small sapling trees? (The trees wait all winter until the warmth of the following spring to begin growing – if they make it that is, many perish along the way!) Although we encourage the children to be mindful of not killing the seeds at Forest School in order to develop a sense of stewardship, sycamore is in fact a naturalized tree in the UK, having arrived here in the 1500s. It can in some sensitive locations become a nuisance, with its many seeds taking over the place of other native trees, so is often removed. However, in parks or woodlands that have had to adapt and change due to development, and in its natural range, it is a wonderful tree that also has many uses, such as making fires, furniture and musical instruments.

TRY THIS!
If you have a group, write names on launchers so they can be returned to their owner after they have been flown.

WALKING STICKS

This activity celebrates the simple act of walking in nature. Walking take us places that cannot be explored by any other means. It gives us time to reflect and be in the moment, while physical activity quietens the mind, letting us be fully immersed in our surroundings. It allows us to hear the sound of the birds, the buzzing of insects and to catch a flower's fragrance on the wind. Walking across uneven ground, our muscles work hard and our brain makes quick judgements; our bodies and minds become more agile and strong. And best of all, walking gives us the simple joy of an unfolding journey.

Making walking sticks and then using them together offers opportunities to chat, explore and discover all the unpredictable things that nature has to offer, bonding all to the space around them and to each other. It also allows the group to assess risk and practise fine as well as gross motor skills. Enjoying the stroll without rushing to get somewhere, focusing on the journey not the destination, creates ease and carefree happiness, especially on a warm summer's day.

Get ready
Gather everyone together and explain that they are going to make walking sticks that, once made, they will take with them on a walking adventure.

Take your time exploring the woodland to find the perfect sticks. Each child needs a stick that's roughly 3cm (1¼in) in diameter and reaches from the ground to about elbow height (sticks can be trimmed to size), with a V-shaped notch at the top. The diameter measurement is only a guide, but bear in mind that the palm drill needs to go through the top of the stick to make a handle (showing the length of the palm drill can be helpful here).

Get set

Show the children how to use the loppers, potato peelers (or sheath knife) and palm drills (see pages 12–14 for tool safety instructions).

LOCATION	Woodland or large natural spaces with fallen sticks
AGE GROUP	4 years +
LEARNING ABOUT...	Being active and healthy ⊛ gross and fine motor skills ⊛ being calm ⊛ focus ⊛ nature connections ⊛ teamwork ⊛ tool use ⊛ risk assessment and management ⊛ creativity

KIT	⇢ Loppers	(one pair per person)
	⇢ Potato peelers or sheath knives (one per person)	⇢ Palm drills
		⇢ Scissors
		⇢ String
	⇢ Gardening gloves	

OPTIONAL	⇢ Marker pens that work on wood, print-outs of Aboriginal stick art or similar for design ideas

To encourage risk assessment and deeper recollection of techniques, it's helpful to ask children that have used tools before to tell you the safety steps before they begin.

Go!

Allow older kids judged capable to have a go under close adult supervision at using all the tools, assisting anyone who needs it.

Trimming Longer sticks can be cut to size with loppers (without wearing gardening gloves) and any branches trimmed to create the V-shaped notch if needed; lay the stick on the ground and use the loppers to remove the excess.

Stripping bark Holding the stick in a gloved hand, and cutting away from the body, use the potato peeler or knife to strip off the bark. Some children may want to remove all the bark, others may just want to remove sections or none at all – it's up to the makers to decide. A potato peeler is safer for younger children; older, capable kids can use a sheath knife (see safety, page 12–13).

Drilling Once the bark has been removed, drill a hole through the walking stick just below the V-shaped notch (see top image, opposite page). Holding the walking stick in one gloved hand, brace it on the ground and twist the palm drill in a clockwise direction to bore a hole through the stick. Keep all helper hands away from the drill in case it bounces out of the hole (anyone helping steady the stick should also wear gloves as extra protection). Once through, simply twist the drill in the opposite direction to remove it.

Stringing Makers should now cut a piece of string long enough to go through the hole and around their wrist – this will be the walking stick handle. Thread one end of the string through the hole and, once through, tie both ends with an overhand knot – great for making a secure fixed loop. To do this, line up both ends of your cord and make a loop with the doubled-up cord. Thread the free ends through the loop and pull tight to create a fixed loop of the desired size (see image, below right).

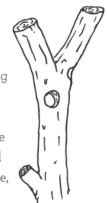

Decorating Now, if the makers wish, they can decorate their walking sticks using coloured pens. Maybe they would like to draw patterns of dots like those found in some Australian Aboriginal art, or stars or squiggly lines . . . it's completely up to them. Have a look at each other's designs and see how amazing and unique they all are.

Exploring Now it's time to head off into the surrounding area – who knows what you will discover along the way!

Endings

At the end of your journey, you could talk about what everyone discovered. How did the children like having their very own walking stick? What did they like best about the stick – making it, using it, keeping it? Was there anything they found tricky or would do differently next time? You could talk about how some wood types – ash, holly and lime – are good for working with but dryer and harder wood types can be more difficult to work with.

SUMMER DAY OUT

The thought of summer often conjures
up childhood memories of delicious picnics,
rolling down grassy hills and playing in the trees – all
perfect activities for Forest School! With plenty of space
and wild foods ripe for picking, whole days drift easily
by without a word about wanting to leave. This summer
day out encompasses the joy of eating outside, sharing
games and creating art that taps into the bounty of
nature that is all around us at this time of year.

Plum trees (*Prunus domestica*) can be found along some of our
Forest School trails, and the children now know to be on the watch
as the beautiful spring flowers turn to juicy fruits in the summer.
This means not only fresh plums to eat, but a chance to make all
sorts of tasty chutneys, pies and – one of the favourites – stewed
fruit crumble. To accompany the humble yet delicious plum, we
add sweet ripe blackberries (*Rubus spp*), another of the children's
wild food favourites, and wash it all down with a cup of red clover
tea – a taste of summer in a cup! From June to September, red
clover (*Trifolium pratense*) turns patches of grass purple-crimson
as the sweet flowers (irresistible to bees) explode into being. The
children love to search for the lucky
four-leafed ones!

Foraging for plums and blackberries
to make crumble, and red clover for
making tea, teaches children how to

LOCATION	Woodland sites that allow fires are ideal, but other natural outdoor spaces where there is wild food to gather and a place to make fire will work too
AGE GROUP	4 years +
LEARNING ABOUT ...	✿ Plant identification ✿ sustainability ✿ nature connections ✿ nutrition ✿ hygiene ✿ gross and fine motor skills ✿ history ✿ self-reliance ✿ confidence ✿ community and team work ✿ trust ✿ belonging ✿ risk assessment and management ✿ independence ✿ self-esteem ✿ listening skills ✿ patience ✿ focus ✿ strategic thinking ✿ being healthy and active ✿ social skills ✿ self-regulation ✿ creativity ✿ imagination ✿ communication
SAFETY	RED CLOVER has many claimed health benefits, including acting as an anti-inflammatory and an immune booster, and as such is considered safe taken in amounts commonly found in food. However, in large quantities red clover can act like oestrogen and disrupt important hormonal balances, so it is best avoided during pregnancy, breastfeeding or alongside treatment for oestrogen-related illnesses. As always, if taking any medication and/or in doubt, please check with your doctor.
FLOW OF THE DAY	See page 45

identify these plants and understand that they change through the seasons. Learning that many species rely on these food sources deepens an understanding of ecology and the sustainable use of resources, connecting the children more closely to the natural world.

Collecting wild food and cooking on an open fire develops fine motor skills, encourages good hygiene and raises awareness of nutrition. It is a truly ancient activity that links us directly to our hunter-gathering past – the children love to think about this and experience it with all their senses. We have seen at our own Forest School how learning where wild food can be found increases the children's sense of self-reliance and confidence, and collecting food together and sharing it creates a sense of community, deepening trust and a sense of belonging. Working with fire under adult supervision is a responsible task that requires children to listen, be patient and focus, as well as assess risk, which in turn develops independence and raises self-esteem.

Animal Tag is great for running off energy, and using strategic thinking as the children swerve and dash around to avoid capture. It's a wonderful bonding game that develops social skills, confidence and self-reliance. The children share lots of laughs as well as their love of animals, as the game encourages them to think about the wildlife that lives locally to them and where the game is being held as well as elsewhere in the world, creating nature connections and furthering a sense of belonging. And in a game that has no "losers", it provides an opportunity to work through any feelings of disappointment in a safe environment.

TRY THIS!
If children haven't formed friendships yet, allocate teams for activities so no one feels left out.

Once the children have had a good run around, Mandala Art gives them the opportunity to create unique pieces of art that express ideas, feelings, creativity and imagination from natural objects found in the space around them. Showcasing these pieces develops communication skills, builds trust, raises self-esteem and confidence. A perfect end to a summer day out.

Activity 1:
BLACKBERRY AND PLUM CRUMBLE WITH RED CLOVER TEA

Get ready

Set up your base at the designated fire site, then head off to forage. Most open spaces should have red clover and blackberries, but if you think finding plums will prove difficult, you could always bring these along with you. Make sure everyone in the group knows what they will be picking, ideally showing them a sample. Everyone needs to gather roughly a cup of blackberries and two handfuls of plums each. Half a cup of clover flowers will do for each cup of tea.

Get set

Now you will need a fire for cooking. Gather dry sticks in a range of sizes: matchstick-size for tinder (dry grasses and shed tree bark works well too); a bundle of finger-sized sticks for kindling; and larger sticks, from arm thickness up to full logs, for the main fire fuel. Ensure you have enough wood to feed your fire for the duration of your cooking. Once you have enough of everything, head back to the base.

TRY THIS!
Avoid wood from elder, yew or rhododendron trees as they release toxic fumes when burned, as well as green wood, which creates lots of smoke

Now is a good time to remind everyone of the fire safety rules (see page 15). Children can help out with the different stages if they wish, always under adult supervision.

KIT	→ Containers to collect fruit and flowers
	→ Firewood (if dry sticks are not available on site), cotton wool, Vaseline, fire steel, lighters or matches and fire safety kit (see page 15)
	→ Sieve (for washing fruit)
	→ 2 x fireproof saucepans
	→ Water (for cooking and washing hands and fruit)
	→ Cups (2 per person)
	→ Wooden spoon (for stirring)
	→ Spoons (1 per person)
	→ Whipped or pouring cream
	→ Digestive biscuits
OPTIONAL	→ Newspaper, plums (if not available locally) or pre-made plum stew, honey, mint, blanket to sit on, fire bowl with grill

Go!

Making fire in the fire pit or bowl First, take a ball of cotton wool and tease out the fibres; this creates an easier ignition point. You can also add a base of twisted newspaper first on which to lay the cotton wool. Dab a smear of Vaseline onto the cotton wool with your finger. This helps the fire start and the flame last longer. Arrange the kindling in a tipi shape over the added tinder and cotton wool, leaving a space through which to light it.

Kneel on one knee rather than two when striking, as this allows you to move easily away from the fire if you need to. Now hold the fire steel, lighter or match firmly, just above the cotton wool or to one side of it and strike it alight. An adult can do this or a capable child under supervision. Now let the small twigs burn, adding progressively larger pieces of wood as the fire gets going. Again, the children can help with this so long as an adult is supervising closely. Remember to use fire-resistant gloves. An adult must watch the fire at all times while it is alight.

TRY THIS!
If you cannot locate a site that allows fire, you could always pre-make the fruit stew and let children add some fresh blackberries to it. Remember to bring a flask of hot water for the tea!

Cooking While the fire burns down slightly to coals, prepare your food. Wash hands, flowers and fruit. With fire-resistant gloves, place a saucepan of water on the coals for the tea. As the water heats up, place about half a cup of fresh red clover blossoms in each of the cups. Squeeze out the plum stones and put the plums and blackberries into the other saucepan. Pour over just enough water to cover the base of the pan, to prevent the fruit from burning and to make the stew more juicy. Place the second pan on the coals.

Stir the fruit as it heats up for roughly 10 minutes until it resembles a stew (the fruit should be soft and breaking apart). Now remove the pan from the heat and allow the contents to cool down. Older, capable children can do all of these stages themselves.

Steeping and finishing: While the fruit cools, pour the hot water over the flowers (best for an adult to do this) and let the tea steep for about 10 minutes. The children can now spoon out the stewed fruit into the base of a cup, crumble over some digestive biscuits and add cream on top of it all. Our groups love the cream you get in aerosol form but if you prefer you can use pouring cream. Clover flowers have a natural sweetness to them so taste great as they are but honey or mint can also be added to the tea (especially good if anyone has a cold!). Now it's time to tuck in to the taste of summer. Delicious!

Endings

You could ask the children if they liked their wild food – if so, why? Did they like making a fire to cook on? Ask them to talk through the safety procedures they would use for another fire, to help embed this in their memory. Do they know that clover leaves can be eaten on their own and are also good in salads, soups and cooked like spinach. Remind them also that wild food should only be gathered and eaten when the plant can be positively identified. It's interesting to talk about this plant's long history of use in many cultures. In Europe, it is now used as cattle feed and as a fertilizer, but in medieval times it was used as a medicine for healing respiratory diseases. At that time, it was believed that anyone who found and carried a four-leaf clover would be able to see fairies! When clover was introduced to America by the first settlers, Native American cultures swiftly adopted the plant into their herb lore and diets. The Pomo tribes of California even have a special clover feast and dance to celebrate its return each year.

Activity 2: ANIMAL TAG

Get ready

Use your six cones (or some other markers, such as bags) to mark out a large, trip-free rectangle on the ground. This will be the playing area, so make it wide and long enough to be challenging for your group to run from one end to the other, but not so big that it's impossible for the middle player to catch the others.

Get set

Explain that the two short ends of the playing area are the home bases, where players cannot be caught. In the middle of the playing area will be a tagger – this is the player that tries to catch the other players as they run from one side to another.

All the other players now line up, shoulder to shoulder, at one end of the pitch. Everyone thinks of an animal, without letting anyone else know what their animal is. They must stick to their choice throughout the game.

Go!

TRY THIS!
Once you've explained how the game works, have a trial run to check everyone understands before starting to play for real.

The tagger stands in the middle of the pitch and asks questions that will help them identify which animals the other players have chosen. For example: "Does your animal have fur?" "Does it live in the sea?" "Is it a reptile?" If the player can answer "yes" to any of the tagger's questions, they must run

| KIT | → 6 small cones (other items such as bags can also be used if you have no cones) |

from one side of the pitch to the other. They can be caught by the tagger on the way but cannot be tagged once "home" at the other end of the pitch. Those that make it should wait at home base until more questions are asked and all players come to join them. Those that are caught are not out, but join the middle player and become taggers too. They can now also ask questions with their new teammates. The game carries on until all animals have been caught.

Adults referee along with anyone else who may not want to play (perhaps because they feel tired or nervous). We find that all the laughs and fun strategic playing created by this game usually coaxes referees into joining in.

When everyone has been tagged, ask them what their animals were – they'll usually be bursting at the seams to tell!

Endings

You could ask each child to tell everyone why they chose their particular animal. Did anyone work out what the other players' animals were? What did they all like best about the game? If they'd like to play again, perhaps this time they could choose an animal that might be found in the local area. This will encourage them to connect more deeply with their immediate natural surroundings.

Activity 3: MANDALA

Get ready

In this activity, a mandala made with sticks on the gound acts as a canvas for creating natural art. The idea is to outline a mandala in the shape of an old-fashioned cartwheel, with spokes that divide the mandala into sections, and then decorate each section with found natural objects. The children will need to collect enough long sticks (about the length of a leg or longer) to create a mandala with a section of the wheel for each child. With large groups, the players can choose whether they'd like to work in groups, sharing a section of the wheel with others, or construct an extra mandala so that everyone can have a section of their own.

Get set

Once the mandala shape is created, the children head off into the surrounding area to find items for their own personal artwork, free to choose whatever stands out to them. Maybe they will collect leaves, feathers, mud, stones, even litter (if it's safe) . . . it's up to them. Remind them, though, to keep their foraging to the forest floor, so as to conserve the natural habitat.

Go!

Once they have their items, they can create their art in a section of the mandala on the floor. The artwork can represent whatever they

KIT	→ Long sticks (if fallen ones are not available)

want it to, whether that be a story, a memory, a feeling, something they have seen – anything at all they would like to make and perhaps show the rest of the group.

Some very beautiful, even funny pieces of work have been created in our Forest School sessions. One memorable example was a mini troll's house made from rocks, mud and moss. The troll himself was a clay ball collected from a nearby stream – he fitted the scene as he had a faint smell of decaying leaves about him! But he was a happy soul that loved his house and would defend it come what may!

Endings

Tell everyone how amazing their work is. Ask if anyone wants to talk about their work with the group. If so, ask them why they chose to make their particular piece of art – did anything in the forest trigger an idea? When they were looking for their materials, did they find they noticed their surroundings more? Did they look more closely than usual at what they found? If so, what did they notice? If anyone is too shy to share their work in a group, it may help to ask them when they are alone if they want to talk about what their art represents with you, or take a photo for later.

Autumn

Now the sun sits lower in the sky and the days are getting shorter. The green of the trees' leaves is breaking down to reveal a host of radiant colours: intense yellows, vivid reds, deep oranges and rusty browns. Fall's splendour is broadcast; autumn is upon us. This is a wonderful time of year, with nature providing so many new colours, objects and experiences to explore. Our autumn adventures include trying to creep unheard across crispy leaves, storytelling on wet days, and collecting fruit and nuts to eat or natural objects to transform into art.

The changeable weather of this season keeps us on our toes. Saying that, we have had some of our most heart-warming experiences on wet autumn days. On one such day, the clouds suddenly turned a dark grey and the heavens opened. The children seized the moment and began joyfully splashing in puddles and catching raindrops in their mouths, before finally taking shelter to watch the deluge wash the trees clean.

It was the perfect opportunity for story stones. With water splashing all around them, the children created a tale about a magical rabbit who, together with his pirate friend, sailed across the rolling ocean waves in search of treasure. The trove of gold and jewels they'd been seeking was long gone, but they discovered the true treasure was their friendship. Inspired!

STORY STONES

Human beings were telling tales long before they knew how to write them down. In fact, storytelling has always been a feature of human existence, ensuring ancient wisdom, local traditions and the knowledge of historical events survived throughout the ages. Cultures across the world have developed their own styles of communicating these stories, many drawing on poetry, music, song or chanting to enhance the effect. In this way, stories travel down through the generations – just think of all the myths and legends, some created millennia ago, that are still well known today.

This activity allows for the creation of new epic tales. With no script to follow, the children transport themselves to all sorts of far-flung places to encounter extraordinary characters and eye-opening situations. Story stones can be used whenever you like, but some of our best experiences have been on wet days, huddled all together under a shelter, when the rain doesn't allow for fair-weather crafts and games to be played.

Storytelling can help children find their voices and develop communication skills, which in turn can boost confidence. This activity offers a real workout for the imagination and creative abilities. Taking turns and remembering a storyline allows children to develop their memory, patience, focus, empathy and listening skills, as well as expanding vocabulary. The story can also be a safe

LOCATION	Any natural outdoor space
AGE GROUP	3 years +
LEARNING ABOUT ...	⊛ Communication ⊛ confidence ⊛ imagination ⊛ creativity ⊛ memory ⊛ patience ⊛ focus ⊛ empathy ⊛ listening skills ⊛ vocabulary ⊛ self-awareness ⊛ emotional intelligence ⊛ trust ⊛ community
KIT	→ Smooth, round, palm-size pebbles (one per person) → Drawstring bag (or similar), to hold the stones 〵 →Colouring pens that work on stone (several of each colour for large groups)
OPTIONAL	Biscuits or similar snack, shelter tarps (if rain due), tarps (or similar) to sit on

way of delving into and expressing emotions, while learning how to understand and empathize with the characters increases emotional intelligence and self-awareness. And of course, sitting together to create a tale is a wonderful way of bonding a group.

We delight in remembering the brilliant tales that spontaneously evolved using story stones on our Forest School adventures. Get ready to enter a world of wonder and make some happy memories!

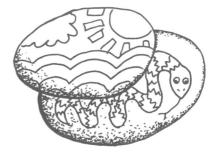

Get ready

Before you start, place the pebbles in the bag, and put down a tarp if the ground is damp. Ask everyone to sit down in a circle, placing colouring pens around the inside of the circle so they are within easy reach. Explain that this isn't just any old circle, but a magical storytelling circle that will transport everyone on a special journey.

Get set

Walk around the outside of the circle, asking each child to take a pebble from the bag without looking. Tell them to let their hand guide them to the pebble that feels right for them. When they have their pebble, they can spend a few moments getting to know it by taking note of its shape, colour, texture and weight.

Each child now draws or writes something on their stone. This could be an animal, a pattern, a word – anything they wish. When the stones are finished, the children put them back in the bag. Then shake the bag to mix up the stones.

Go!

Now for the storytelling. Start with someone who's keen to speak and reassure everyone else they will get a turn, too. Ask them to pull a stone out of the bag, look at the picture and use it as inspiration to start a story. When they've finished speaking, they place the stone in the middle of the circle. The storytelling then passes to the next child around the circle, and so on, so that each child gets a chance to choose a stone from the bag and add to the unfolding story. As each child finishes, they add their stone to the line of pebbles inside the circle. Assist anyone who is shy. Once the last person has ended the story and placed their pebble next to the others, everyone stands up to look at the stones in their particular order. Celebrate how wonderful each stone is, and the magical tale they told as a whole, and let everyone know they are welcome to take their pebble home if they wish to.

TRY THIS!
For anyone feeling insecure about inventing a story, handing out biscuits (call them "magic story biscuits") can help give them ideas and a voice to join in.

Endings

Talk about each individual stone – why was that particular picture or word chosen? Discuss the story and what the children's favourite parts were. It's also interesting to think about storytellers from days gone by. In the past, they had an important position in society, as keepers of different cultures. Viking storytellers, for example, who were known as skalds, memorized tales of the Norse gods and goddesses and conveyed them to those they met. These stories were passed down from generation to generation, even to the present day. Who hasn't heard of Thor?

PEG CARVING

We often need hand-carved wooden tent pegs at this time of year, when conventional metal pegs have a habit of slipping out of the wet ground. It's also useful, if you have none to hand, to be able to carve pegs to hitch up a tarp as a shelter from the rain. Strong as well as light, these wooden pegs are also biodegradable, so you don't have to worry if you accidentally leave one behind.

Peg carving is a brilliant way to teach children how to use a knife safely and the pegs can then be used over and over again for an activity like den building that takes place on a regular basis. For these reasons, it is a classic Forest School activity. Knifework offers opportunities for children to assess and manage risks for themselves, which in turn raises self-motivation, independence and confidence. Practising carving with a knife embeds the knowledge that this is a tool to be used and looked after appropriately. As knives can be tricky to use, peg carving is a great chance to practise fine motor skills and encourages the children's focus, patience, perseverance and ability to manage their feelings. If you are seeking out specific types of wood, this activity also teaches children how to identify different trees and their sustainable use.

Whenever we do this activity, the children quickly become engrossed in the task at hand. It's wonderful

LOCATION	Woodland or wooded parkland
AGE GROUP	6 years +
LEARNING ABOUT ...	✿ Risk assessment ✿ self-motivation ✿ independence ✿ confidence ✿ empathy ✿ focus ✿ patience ✿ perseverance ✿ self-regulation ✿ tree identification ✿ nature connections ✿ sustainability ✿ pride ✿ self-esteem
KIT	⇢ Loppers ⇢ Sheath knives (one per person) ⇢ Gardening gloves (one pair per person)
OPTIONAL	⇢ Mallet

to witness their achievement and how they are simply overjoyed – brimming with pride! – when they can use their finished pegs. Their self-esteem is boosted and a new "can-do" attitude is impossible to miss.

Get ready

For each peg you will need a stick roughly 20cm (8in) long, with a diameter of about 2.5cm (1in) (roughly the size of a UK two-pence piece or a US quarter). You can make a peg out of any straight piece of wood, but we tend to use hazel (*Corylus avellana*), ash (*Fraxinus excelsior*), sycamore (*Acer pseudoplatanus*), sweet chestnut (*Castanea sativa*) and holly (*Ilex aquifolium*). If you will be identifying specific types of wood, show the children a picture or sample before you start so they can find suitable pieces. Otherwise, use whatever is in the area. Green wood is easier to carve, especially for beginners (seek permission from the landowner if you intend to cut from trees).

Demonstrate how to use loppers (see pages 12–14) to cut stems to size: wearing no gloves, place the blade around the branch and push the handles together to make a clean cut. Always cut in front of a bark collar or ridge on branches to ensure the tree can heal. Keep a close eye on any children trying this for themselves.

Get set

Once you have cut your sticks, show the group how to make a peg using the sheath knife, again demonstrating safe tool use (see pages 12–14). Sit down, preferably off the ground, and hold the stick to one side of your body in a gloved hand. Hold the unsheathed knife firmly with the ungloved hand in a strong forehand grip. Keeping all limbs out of the way and cutting away from the body, use the knife to make a blunt point on the stick tip. This doesn't need to be really pointed; pegs with blunt tips are less likely to snap when they are driven into the ground. If one end of the stem is thicker than the other, work on the thinner end, leaving the thicker one to be the end for hammering. Keep the gloved hand well away from the cutting edge as you work.

Trim away any bumps on the stick. To avoid the wood splitting when the peg is driven into the ground, gently chamfer away the top edge of this section (see illustration, page 102).

Now make a notch in one side of the peg (nearer to the hammering end), for the rope, cord or string from your tent or tarp to latch onto. To do this, first make a stop cut by placing the blade horizontally on the peg roughly 5cm (2in) from the top, then rock the knife from side to side to make a 1cm (½in) slight slit or indentation in the wood. This will stop your next cut moving past this point and form the top part of your notch. Now take the blade about 3cm (1¼in) down from the slit and start to cut into the wood toward the stop cut (see illustration, page 102). Cut enough away to allow your cord to catch onto the notch that develops and not slip off.

Go!

Demo peg done, now it's time for everyone to have a go. Tell everyone to start working at their own pace, keeping a close eye on each child but only helping when needed. Stress to everyone that they must stay focused on their knifework even when talking! We often find that the children are so happy to be trusted with these tools that they set about the task with real care. A calm state usually falls upon the group while they carve, which is followed by an immense sense of achievement when they see the fruits of their labours.

As soon as the peg is complete, they will probably want to hammer it into the ground – just to check it works properly! You can do this using a mallet if you have one or, if not, a small log will work just as well.

Endings

Explain to the children how they might be able to use their pegs
to build dens or a shelter (like the one on page 148). It's worth
talking through the safe working practices so that these are firmly
embedded in everyone's memory for next time. Discuss, for example,
why it's important to cut away from the body and never leave tools
lying around. Someone may point out that their hands ache after all
that carving, giving an opportunity to explain that this is tough work
that uses muscles in our hands in ways that we are not used to in
everyday life. The more we do it, the less they will ache. You might
like to talk about what the children enjoyed about carving and how
it made them feel. What did they notice about the type of wood they
were using? Do they know what tree it came from? Did it feel soft or
hard? Questions like this may
make them want to experiment
with different types of wood
on this or another
carving adventure!

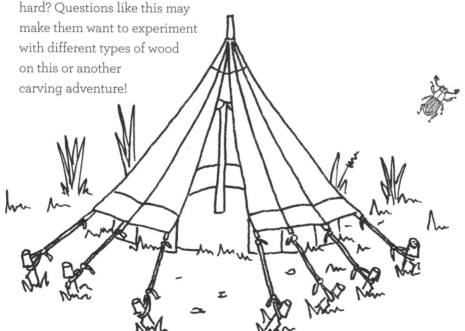

EVERGREEN PAINTBRUSH

As leaves slowly turn to orange and brown and then fall to the ground in autumn, it is the evergreen trees, with their splash of green, that begin to stand out in the crowd. Unlike deciduous trees, whose branches become bare as they shed their foliage for winter's sleep, evergreens remain dressed throughout the year, renewing their leaves only gradually as they are lost.

At Forest School, we like to use the narrow, needle-like leaves of conifers such as pine and spruce to make paintbrushes, but try whatever evergreens are local to your area. Not only do these brushes work well for any budding artist, they are a sensory treat, too. As one child in our group pointed out when using pine leaves: "Mmm . . . minty fresh!"

This is a great activity that gets children using their bodies to the full as they energetically collect leaves and then employ all their dexterity to make the brushes. Patience, perseverance, self-belief and a sense of independence grow as they work to finish the brush, while using something they've created to make art fires up the imagination and allows creativity to flow. Any feelings of disappointment that come up can be explored, developing self-regulation skills, while sharing a piece of work can boost confidence

LOCATION	Woodland or other natural spaces that have evergreen trees
AGE GROUP	3 years +
LEARNING ABOUT ...	❀ fine motor skills ❀ communication ❀ nature connections ❀ plant identification ❀ sensory experiences ❀ imagination ❀ creativity ❀ patience ❀ self-regulation ❀ confidence ❀ self-belief ❀ independence
KIT	⇢ Secateurs ⇢ Paper ⇢ Scissors ⇢ Water and plastic ⇢ String, twine or cup (to clean craft wire brushes in) ⇢ Child-safe paint ⇢ Paint trays
OPTIONAL	⇢ Potato peelers, colouring pens, rubber bands, wire cutters, pegs (to hang pictures to dry), wet wipes

and trust. And, at the end of the day, the children have both the artwork and the tool to take home as treasured mementos that may open up all sorts of interesting conversations about the life strategies of plants and different types of tree, as well as giving more opportunities for artistic expression.

Get ready

Set up camp near some evergreen trees. Avoid areas with yew trees as their leaves (and the seeds within the berries) are poisonous. This is especially important for younger ones who are more likely

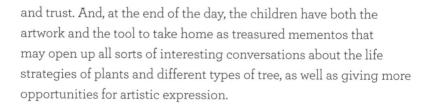

to put their paintbrushes in their mouths! Let everyone know that today they will be able to do some painting. You have the paint and paper – but no paintbrushes. Can anyone see anything around them or think of anything that they might use instead? See if anyone comes up with the idea of using evergreen leaves! The Scots pine (*Pinus sylvestris*) trees that grow on our Forest School sites have needles roughly 2.5–5cm (1–2in) long, which we find work well for making paintbrushes, but you can use what you have locally – just bear in mind your desired size of bristle. Once found, explain to the group that, with these evergreen leaves, they will be able to make a paintbrush of their very own.

Get set

To make the brush handle, everyone needs to find a stick that's roughly the size of a pencil (they can choose one longer or fatter if they wish, so long as they will be able to hold and paint with it).

Once sticks have been found, gather around the evergreen trees. Remind the group that the leaves are precious to the tree and that only a few will be needed for each brush. Using secateurs to make a clean cut, remove a bunch of small side branches from a main branch, taking them from the end of the branch that's closest to the trunk. These hold the older leaves that are likely to be shed when fresh new ones are produced at the tips of the branches. Remember to get the landowner's permission beforehand if needed and don't over-harvest one tree, especially if you are in a large group. Allow enough evergreen leaves per child, so that they can all make one nice bushy paintbrush head (3–4 sprigs works well for Scots pine).

Go!

Some children may want to peel their sticks with a potato peeler (see page 12–14 for safety guidance) and then decorate them with pens. If so, this needs to be done before adding the bristles.

Once the stick is ready, it's time to tie on the heads. Gather up some evergreen leaves and distribute them evenly around the tip of the stick. If the needles are long (over 4cm/1½in), pull them off the stem and pack them around the end of the stick to make the paintbrush head. Tightly tie on the sprigs/needles by wrapping string, twine or craft wire tightly several times around the leaves. If using string, knot the ends together using a straightforward granny knot. If using craft wire, trim with a wire cutter and fold down the tips to avoid sharp ends pointing out. Brush done, it's time to pass out the paints and paper and create a unique piece of art!

Endings

Firstly, admire the wonderful individual paintbrushes and the fabulous art the children have produced. Ask them whether they enjoyed making their brushes and why. Did they notice any other evergreen trees in the area? If yes, do they look the same as the one they used for their paintbrushes? Talk about deciduous trees, which shed all their leaves during the autumn months, and evergreen trees, which renew their leaves gradually. This might be after a few months or, in the case of the Great Basin bristlecone pine (*Pinus longaeva*), an epic 45 years!

TRY THIS!
If younger children struggle tying on leaves, put a rubber band at the top of the stick for them to push leaves under. An adult can then tightly secure the head with string or wire.

CREEPING COYOTE

The word "coyote" is a Mexican-Spanish term of Aztec origin, meaning "trickster". This really suits the clever coyote, who walks on tiptoes to sneak up on its prey – invaluable traits for this game! We have seen how the children race ahead, dying to be the first to reach the target, only to find that the cracking of sticks and leaves has given them away. Instead, quiet stealth, like that of the coyote, is required. It's a perfect game for autumn, when the forest floor is littered with twigs and leaves.

This active game is great for practising balance and movement, and there's also a lot of strategic thinking, independence, patience

LOCATION	Deciduous woodland, with lots of fallen leaves and twigs, is ideal
AGE GROUP	4 years +
LEARNING ABOUT ...	⊛ Gross motor skills ⊛ patience ⊛ perseverance ⊛ focus ⊛ strategic thinking ⊛ nature connections ⊛ self-regulation ⊛ independence ⊛ confidence ⊛ trust ⊛ belonging ⊛ sensory experiences
NUMBER OF PLAYERS	3 +
KIT	→ Blindfold

and perseverance involved. Having to go back to the start if heard creeping up can allow children to work through feelings of disappointment in a supported playful atmosphere, building self-regulation skills. The blindfolded player, meanwhile, learns about staying focused, confident and trusting, and puts their listening skills to good use. Thinking about the clever coyote also opens up curiosity about different animal-survival strategies.

Get ready

Mark out the boundary of your stalking area (dragging a stick across the ground should do it). There needs to be lots of fallen leaves and twigs on the ground – under a deciduous tree is ideal. The space must be large enough for the players to stand in a circle around the middle blindfolded player, but not so large that the middle player cannot hear them.

Get set

Choose the player to be blindfolded. (To make a random selection, see the "Try This" suggestion on p.69.) The chosen player then selects a stick – this is what the coyote players around the circle will try to steal.

Go!

Players take up their positions. The coyotes stand in a circle around the blindfolded player, who has their stick at their feet. Wait until everyone is quiet, then begin the countdown: three, two, one – Go!

The coyotes now try to creep up, take the special stick and get back to their starting point without being heard by the blindfolded player. The blindfolded player listens hard and points in the direction of any noise; if anyone is caught out they have to go back to their starting point and try again. The pointing doesn't have to be precise – just close enough. See how everyone works out their best strategies. Some might think rushing will work, while others may move slow and steady. Others may wait until someone else moves and then go with them to disguise their own footsteps.

The winner is the coyote who manages to pick up the stick and get back to the starting point without being heard! You can then play another round, choosing a different blindfolded player.

Endings

How did it feel for the blindfolded player, having to rely on hearing alone? Talk about the tactics used by all the players and which ones seemed to work best. Were there any team strategies in which players cooperated? Interestingly, coyotes have been known to hunt as a team with American badgers, working together to help each other to dig up rodent prey – this is called a mutualistic relationship. Can anyone think of any other benefits to working as a team?

AUTUMN'S RAINBOW

Colour is all around us. We see it every day, but most of us are too busy and distracted to stop and admire it. Colour plays a vital role in the natural world, from the magnificent shades that flowers use to guide pollinators to their nectar, to the warning hues of insects, such as the striking red and black colouring of the humble ladybird. Yet, whether we notice it consciously or not, the colours we see in nature from day to day affect our outlook, too. They can also act as a powerful trigger of memories.

This was evident when a boy on one of our autumn Forest School excursions picked up a bright yellow leaf that had fallen from a black locust (*Robinia pseudoacacia*) tree and said: "This reminds me of the yellow lollipop I had at my friend's party." He then exclaimed: "Wish I had that now!", swiftly followed by a yellow-lolly victory dance, which was so infectious it swept us all along for the ride, throwing handfuls of fallen leaves as we went!

This fallen-leaf activity is both active and creative, and provides a space for children to explore the full array of autumn colour – fading greens, deep purples, vibrant reds and oranges, intense yellows and rusty browns. Stirring up mud (and getting muddy), looking at the colours and feeling

LOCATION	Mixed deciduous woodland with a range of colourful fallen leaves is ideal
AGE GROUP	3 years +
LEARNING ABOUT ...	Being active ⊛ creativity ⊛ gross and fine motor skills ⊛ sensory experiences ⊛ nature connections ⊛ patience ⊛ focus ⊛ perseverance ⊛ self-belief ⊛ independence ⊛ communication ⊛ trust ⊛ empathy ⊛ community
KIT	⇾ Small bucket (or similar), to carry water
OPTIONAL	⇾ Trowels, water, hand-washing kit (if none available)

the textures of the leaves are all sensory experiences that deepen the children's connection to the natural world. Creating their own colour structures requires patience, focus, perseverance, self-belief and independence. Sharing the artworks with the group develops communication, trust, empathy and a sense of community. And, best of all, the finished rainbows are simply beautiful to see.

Get ready

Choose a spot in woodland with multi-coloured leaves on the ground, ideally with a nearby water source, such as stream or pond (if there isn't one, you'll have to bring water for mud mixing with you). Ask the group to name all the colours in a rainbow. Which of these colours do they think would be in an autumn rainbow and can they see any of these around them in the leaves? Explain to the group how they can make their own autumn rainbow by choosing a range of colourful fallen leaves and carefully attaching them with mud to a low branch or another place of their choosing.

Get set

Let the children explore the area and find their ideal spot for making an autumn rainbow. Perhaps it will be an interestingly twisted branch or a sun-lit fallen log, where the light catches the colours of the leaves. Or, instead of a typical rainbow shape, they might like to make a circle of leaves on a large rock. If there's a group, some may decide to share a location and work together.

Go!

Once everyone has found their chosen natural canvas, it's time to mix some mud! If there's a water source nearby, the children can collect the water for mud mixing in a container, then dig shallow holes in the ground using a trowel or stick. Pour in some water and start mixing up some glorious sticky mud. (If the water drains quickly through the ground, they could always mix the mud in the container.)

Reassure anyone who's worried about getting dirty that it's okay to get muddy and that they can wash (or at least wipe) their hands whenever they need to. Ask the children to grab some mud with their hands or the trowel and sculpt the rainbow outline.

Mud outline made, everyone gathers up some leaves that show the changing colours of autumn and push these into this mud in whatever order the makers choose to create their own idea of an autumn rainbow. Once they're all complete, stand back and admire the colourful view with rainbows all around!

Endings

Invite the children to share their thoughts and ideas about their rainbow. Which part of the activity did they like best? Was it squeezing the sticky mud? Collecting leaves? Running around? Would they do anything different next time? Do the children have any ideas about why most deciduous trees drop their leaves in the autumn? In fact, it's to save energy. Trees can sense changes in light thanks to chemical receptors in their leaves. These clever leaves also have a green-coloured pigment called chlorophyll that absorbs sunlight and turns it into food, some of which gets stored for winter. As sunlight fades, the tree senses this change, and chlorophyll production eventually stops. The green pigment begins to disappear from the leaf, allowing others that were previously hidden in the greenery to appear: the reds, yellows, oranges and browns we see during this season. As winter approaches, these fading soft leaves that can be damaged are shed to conserve energy, leaving only the trees' toughest parts – its stems, branches and trunk – to brave the cold and windy months ahead. Smart!

AUTUMN DAY OUT

The days may be getting shorter, chillier and wetter, but autumn days out are magical. With piles of multicoloured leaves to kick in the air, fruit tumbling from trees and squirrels busy storing nuts, there's something to catch the eye wherever you look. Leaves, fruits and nuts that were previously out of reach high in the trees are now readily found on the forest floor, opening up a whole new world to explore.

Apples and nuts are ready for picking in autumn, so this day out includes a delicious recipe for baked apples stuffed with fruit and nuts. We are lucky to have apple trees near our Forest School sites, and enjoy picking the fruit when it's ripe. Nuts, however, can be harder to come by, so for ease we tend to bring these along with us. This activity gives the children a direct understanding of seasonal change and sustainability, as they learn how flowers, with the help of pollinators, grow into fruits. Foraging food, and then preparing and cooking it, not only requires an understanding of hygiene, planning, patience and risk management, which raises self-esteem and independence, but is among the most bonding of Forest School activities, with conversations naturally arising about the children's likes and dislikes as they work and eat together.

Autumn is a great time for den building, with lots of branches to find on the forest floor after spells of heavy rain and wind. This is another team-building activity, requiring the children to listen, communicate and assess risk as they work as a team, building confidence, empathy

LOCATION	Woodland that allows fire is ideal but outdoor spaces with the materials needed will also do
AGE GROUP	3 years +
LEARNING ABOUT ...	✿ Nature connections ✿ plant identification ✿ sustainability ✿ hygiene ✿ planning ✿ focus ✿ patience ✿ risk assessment and management ✿ sharing ✿ trust ✿ independence ✿ pride ✿ confidence ✿ self-esteem ✿ sense of belonging ✿ being active and healthy ✿ fine and gross motor skills ✿ teamwork ✿ listening skills ✿ communication ✿ mathematics ✿ architecture ✿ knot-tying ✿ self-reliance ✿ empathy ✿ community ✿ creativity
FLOW OF THE DAY	See page 45

See page 45

and a sense of community. They will get plenty of exercise, too! When a shelter is done, it creates a wonderful sense of belonging for the builders. We have often seen how children rush over to the shelters they've built, throwing coats and bags inside as if returning home, readily rebuilding or adding to them – even tidying up!

Stitching leaves is a focused activity that encourages dexterity and creativity, and connects them to the season and their environment. As they work, conversations often occur about why leaves change colour and fall, and the natural cycles of life. The beautiful end result instills a sense of pride and confidence in everyone.

Activity 1: BAKED APPLES

Get ready

Choose a site where fires are allowed; either use the designated fire pit or bring a fire bowl. If you plan to pick apples, remember to get the landowner's permission first. You will need a bundle of tinder (matchstick-size wood, dry grass and tree bark shavings), as well as kindling (twigs and finger-thick wood about the same length as your logs), plus small branches and logs (leave any with mini beasts alone!). The logs should be around 40cm (16in) long and 3cm (1¼in) in diameter. Bring this all with you if it's not available on site.

KIT **To make the** **baked apples:**	→ Bags for collecting apples → Towel or kitchen paper, soap and water to wash hands → Potato peelers (one per person) → Heavy-duty aluminum foil	→ Teaspoons (one per person) → Brown sugar → Chopped walnuts → Raisins → Ground cinnamon → Butter → Spoons (one per person)
To build the **fire:**	→ Firewood (if not on the ground) → Firelighters (matches, fire steel)	→ Tongs → Container of water → Fireproof gloves → Fire blanket
OPTIONAL	→ Fire bowl, cotton wool, Vaseline, apples (one per person, if not available locally), honey, maple syrup	

Before setting out foraging, show the children what an apple tree looks like. When they've identified the trees, get them to pick one apple each, choosing firm, ripe apples (which will be sweet). It's a good idea to take two spares, too, for any potential mistakes. Put them in the bags and head back to your chosen cooking spot.

Get set

A log cabin fire is perfect for baking the apples on, and also particularly good for damp weather as the fire is raised up off the ground. This keeps the wood dry and allows a lot of oxygen to circulate, helping the fire to burn. This fire lay can be constructed in a fire bowl if no permanent pit is available. Before you begin, remind everyone of the fire safety rules (see page 15).

The fire makers should start to build the "log cabin" by placing two logs of roughly equal length parallel to one another on the ground about two adult hand-widths apart. Then they should place two more of the same-sized logs across the ends of the lower logs, making a square shape. Ask them to take some kindling and make a raft across the upper logs. In the middle of this raft, place the tinder and a piece of Vaseline-smeared cotton wool, if you are using this as an ignition point. Now build up the log cabin around the tinder, mirroring the

pattern on the base. Go up a couple more layers and add another raft of kindling across this layer. Continue to build the log cabin up around this for another couple of layers (see illustration on page 121).

Go!

It's time to light the fire! Use a fire steel, a lighter or matches to set fire to the cotton wool or the tinder. If a competent child is helping here, encourage them to kneel on one knee as this is a stable position that allows them to move back quickly if needed. Keep adding wood if required; you shouldn't need much. Once burning, the fire will eventually fold down in the middle and form coals, which is what you want to cook the apples on.

While the fire burns down, prepare your apples. Hands and fruit need to be washed, and everyone needs an apple, a peeler and a piece of aluminum foil. The foil must be big enough to cover the apple with some remaining to make a twisted top that can be grabbed by tongs to move it once it's in the fire.

Demonstrate how to make the dessert. The children can make theirs alongside you as you show each stage. Take a potato peeler and scoop out the core of the apple, leaving a tunnel roughly 2cm (¾in) wide. It's important not to go all the way through the apple, but leave a base at the bottom to hold the filling inside. Sit the apple on top of the foil, then place two teaspoons of brown sugar (or honey/maple syrup) and chopped walnuts inside the apple. Now add one teaspoon of raisins and ¼ teaspoon of cinnamon and place a knob of butter on top. Now wrap the apple in the foil and twist into a point on top.

Once the fire has burnt down to coals, place the apples on to cook. They should be done in 20 minutes. You can check by squeezing them with tongs. If the apple feels soft, it's ready! An adult or an older child can move the apples on and off the fire using fire-resistant gloves.

The foil packages will initially be very hot so let them cool down enough to be handled. Then open them up and hand out the spoons so everyone can enjoy! Let the fire burn down and extinguish before leaving the site. If you have used a fire bowl, spread the wet ash around on the ground and mix with the earth to leave no trace.

Endings

Talk about the delicious baked apples. How might the children change the recipe for next time? Ask them what creatures in your area might eat apples. Squirrels and birds definitely love them! It's also fun to talk about the many different ways to make a fire. The one they made today is known as a log cabin fire lay. Did they think it was good for cooking on? Other than cooking, what benefits might fire bring us? Ideas might include warmth, light, protection from wild animals – also, bugs hate smoke! You might also want to discuss why fire is dangerous. Remind the group that, to avoid these dangers, they should never make fires in places that are not designated for it or without an adult or safety equipment to hand.

Activity 2: DEN BUILDING

For a simple, tipi-shaped den, the children will need to find three long, pole-shaped branches roughly 2–2.5m (7–8ft) in length, that are straight and fairly even in size. Shorter branches can be used, but the den will be smaller and lower. The safest method to move long branches is to hold one end under an arm and drag it along the ground – this way no one gets hit on the head! It's also good to remind everyone that you are all together as one community, so there is no need to get territorial! It's fun to visit one another's dens, or make one big den for everyone.

Get ready

Once you have your branches, trim off any smaller branches protruding from the main pole using loppers (follow the safe working practices on pages 12–14). Loppers can cut branches up to approximately 2.5cm (1in) in diameter. Allow older children to do this under supervision, and assist younger ones where needed.

Now the children can lay the poles parallel to one another, making sure the bottoms of the legs (the thickest ends) are lined up evenly. Try to make the poles lie as close to one another as possible. Cut enough cord to bind the poles together using a tripod lashing (see opposite).

KIT	→ Loppers
	→ String (or cord/thin rope)
	→ Scissors
OPTIONAL	→ Pre-made bramble cordage (see page 27), tarp for flooring

Go!

Get the child who is tying the poles together to kneel down at the top of the poles (the thinner ends) and lay the long (non-working) end of the string across the top of the poles, about 15cm (6in) down from the top. The working (shorter) end of the string closest to them will then be used to tie a clove hitch knot around the nearest pole.

To tie a clove hitch Take the working end of the string (the short end of your string that you are moving) and wrap it around and under the nearest pole. When you bring the string back up, cross it over the non-working end of the string to make an X shape. Take the working end and go underneath the pole again, then bring it back up and tuck it under the top part of the X, next to the non-working end, and pull tight. Your knot is done.

To make a tripod lashing (with plain turns) Now the previous non-working end (the longer part of your string) will become the working end for the tripod lashing, to tie the poles together. Take the long end of the string and wrap it around all three poles six to eight times. Keep these turns tight. When you have done this, take the string in between the middle pole and the pole with the clove hitch and take two frapping turns (wrapping the string around the string). Pull the string back through the two poles and pull tight. Now take the string and wrap it over the middle pole. Come up between the outer pole and the middle pole and apply another two fraps. As the poles are lashed

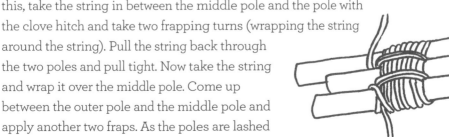

together it can be difficult to get the string in between the poles – here it helps to lift the outer pole slightly out of the way to allow access. When done again, pull them tight. Finish

with another clove hitch round the outer pole close to the other wraps.

To stand up the tipi tripod, cross the outside legs away from the middle pole. The basic structure of the den is now ready to work on.

To make the den more stable, the children can tie on crossbars – two at the bottom about 60cm (2ft) from the floor and three at the top about 60cm (2ft) down from the lashing. Having the higher crossbars lower than the lashing means that any poles added to fill in the den can be shorter than the main ones. Tie the crossbars on with a square lash.

To tie a square lash knot Tie a clove hitch or granny knot on a tipi pole, in the place where you want to attach one end of a crossbar. Lay the end of your chosen crossbar across the top of the tipi pole. The pole and stick should look a bit like a cross shape now with imaginary compass bearings. Bring the long end of the string up and over the east side of the horizontal stick and then under the north side of the vertical stick, then again over the west side of the horizontal stick, and under the south side of the vertical stick. Repeat this pattern five or six times, pulling tightly at each turn to fix the sticks in place. Once complete, take two frapping turns to tighten it all up and finish with a clove hitch or granny knot. Cut any excess string away. One section of

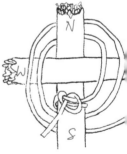

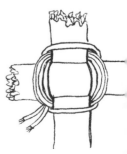

the crossbar is now securely fastened. Do the same for the other end, which will complete one cross bar. Repeat as needed around your den. You could even use pre-made bramble cordage (see page 27) for this part of the activity if you have some!

Now the sides can be filled in with branches and the walls built up with fallen leaves to make the den warm and cozy. Add a tarp for flooring if you have one.

Endings

Stand back and admire the fantastic den or dens. Ask the makers if you can come inside. You could talk about how it feels to have their very own shelter built by themselves. What, if anything, did they find tricky? It's quite likely to be the knots – if so, would they like to practise them again on smaller sticks? This den is similar to a tipi. A traditional tipi would have been made from many poles and animal skins, and would keep you dry in heavy rainfall, cool in summer and warm in the winter when a fire could be built inside! These shelters were used by the people of the Great Plains and Canadian Prairies of North America as well as indigenous Sami peoples of northern Europe and other tribes in Asia.

Activity 3: LEAF STITCHING

Get ready

Invite everyone to gather up the fallen leaves that they would like to stitch together. The makers can choose the leaves that stand out for them: perhaps that will be leaves of the same size and colour or a combination of different colours and sizes. If they want to make a mobile or attach the string of leaves to a stick, they need to find a suitable stick, too.

Get set

Put a tarp down and place all the natural materials, as well as the masking tape, scissors and string, on top of it to create a comfortable setting for the makers to work at their own pace. Each maker can create a needle by wrapping a small piece of masking tape around the end of a length of string. This stiffens the tip of the string and allows it to easily pierce through a leaf.

Go!

The makers can now stitch their leaves with the string. They may want to stitch through one leaf only and make a pattern on it with the string or maybe stitch several leaves together. When the stitching is finished, taping the end of the string to a leaf will prevent it pulling through.

KIT
→ A tarp or equivalent to sit and work on
→ Masking tape
→ Scissors
→ String

Then the children can get creative with their sticks, if they wish. We have seen some wonderful creations – from leaf kites to mobiles of hanging leaves to a leaf dragon, with a face cut by scissors into a large leaf and a tail made of several leaves decreasing in size that trailed behind. It looked amazing as it was whisked through the air by its maker. These creations can also be used to decorate the dens. Let the children decide – you will be amazed!

Endings

Admire each creation. Look at all the different leaves. You may want to talk about the different trees that the leaves come from, as well as about what each creation represents. Join in and make an autumn leaf stitching yourself, asking for tips on what to do. They'll be bursting to help!

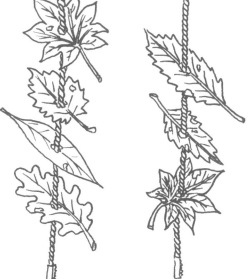

Winter

Don't let the cold weather put you off going outside. We have had so many wonderful winter adventures with our Forest School groups, enjoying muddy tracks, glistening cobwebs and the new perspective fading light brings to the landscape. There's nothing so warming as a winter fire, when the yellow flames light up the darkness and mulled apple juice bubbles away, giving off the warming scent of Christmas spices.

On one occasion, as we sat around a fire, eating food we had prepared and sharing jokes and tales, a girl told us how much she loved winter twilight – how it made her feel calm and the woods seem like something out of a fairy tale. With nodding heads and rounds of "yeah!" whispered out, the whole group agreed. A special moment.

The activities in this chapter are inspired by the natural world in winter, from animal-track casts to a game in which children try to escape a giant-size spider's web. There are crafts to reflect this season's traditions, as well as energetic games plus fire and shelter-building activities to keep everyone warm and dry – essential at this time of year. As, of course, is having fun. So wrap up well, then head out and breathe in the fresh, crisp air. Run around to keep warm and then, when the day is done, eat and rest, restored and in tune with this truly magical season.

ELF CARVING

When children think of elves, it's the mystical little beings with pointy ears and hats who make the Christmas toys at the North Pole that often come to mind. The festive season is a great opportunity for a spot of elf carving. We love to see how the children become fully immersed in this activity, and how thrilled they are with their new skills and the elf characters they create from ordinary sticks!

Knifework encourages children to assess and manage risks for themselves, taking ownership of the process and handling tools mindfully, and offers fantastic benefits in terms of self-motivation, independence, confidence and care for themselves and others. It requires both dexterity and strength, as well as focus, patience, perseverence and calm. This activity also enhances the children's understanding of the different species and types of wood (wet, dry, firm, decomposing). There's an amazing sense of achievement when, after all the hard work, the elf finally appears, raising self-esteem, and then it's all about imaginative play and storytelling.

On one occasion, a passing Basset Hound took a shine to one of the elves the children had lined up together against a big oak tree. The dog carried the elf a short distance and then dropped it, before going on its way. The escapades of this elf were then woven into a woodland adventure acted out by the children and their creations. The elf in question was named Lucky. (We thought this hilarious!)

LOCATION	Woodland or other outdoor natural space that provides the sticks needed
AGE GROUP	6 years +
LEARNING ABOUT ...	⊛ Risk assessment and management ⊛ mindfulness ⊛ self-motivation ⊛ independence ⊛ confidence ⊛ empathy ⊛ tree identification ⊛ sustainability ⊛ nature connections ⊛ fine motor skills ⊛ focus ⊛ patience ⊛ perseverance ⊛ self-regulation ⊛ transferable skills ⊛ pride ⊛ self-esteem ⊛ imagination ⊛ communication ⊛ community
KIT	→ Secateurs → Sheath knives (one per person) → Gardening gloves (one pair per person) → Cotton wool → Non-toxic children's glue, such as PVA → Colouring pens that work on wood
OPTIONAL	→ Wet wipes to clean sticky fingers

Get ready

Each child needs to find a stick to make their elf. They are looking for a fairly straight piece of wood that is rot-free. A length of approximately 25cm (10in) is good for gripping when carving – if desired, this can always be trimmed using secateurs (see tool use pages 12–14). The ideal circumference is roughly 2.5cm (1in), which will allow the stick to be carved without snapping.

Get set

Remind everyone of the safety rules for using a sheath knife (see pages 12–14) and demonstrate each stage of using a knife to carve an elf. Carve sitting down, holding the stick in a gloved hand to one side of your body, with the unsheathed knife held firmly in your (ungloved) carving hand in a forehand grip. Cut away from the body and keep the gloved hand well away from the cutting edge.

Go!

Allow everyone to work at their own pace, helping only where needed, but always keeping a watchful eye on the process.

Carving To carve the elf's hat, you will want to make a blunt-ended point. On the chosen end of the stick, go down 5cm (2in), push the knife slightly into the wood, then carve all the way along the wood to the end, keeping the gloved hand well away from the cutting edge. Do this all the way around the end of the stick to form a pointed hat. It is easy and tempting to carve a really sharp point, but remind everyone not to, as this could be dangerous, and the end does need to be blunt for the pompom to stick on. Once you are happy with the hat you can begin to cut out the face and the brim of the hat.

To define the face and brim of the hat, make a 1mm-deep stop cut at the base of the hat by placing the blade horizontally on the stick and rocking the knife from side to side, turning the stick as you go, until a slight indentation in the wood runs all the way round. Then move the blade about 3.5cm (1½in) down from the brim (stop cut) and start to cut into the wood toward the stop cut, removing the bark and a little of the wood underneath. Work all the way around the stick. You will end up with a clean face, space for the hair and an edge to the hat. For the mouth, make another small stop cut in the centre of the face about 2cm/¾in from the brim. Move the knife down slightly and carve toward the stop cut until a smiley mouth appears.

Decorating Now for the finishing touches! The makers can draw a nose and eyes on the face. The elf's hat can be coloured in festive green or red, or whatever colours the maker likes. Put a dab of glue on the blunt end of the hat and stick on a pompom of cotton wool. Dab more glue under the face and around the hairline to attach cotton wool for a beard and fluffy white hair. There's also the option of carving away some bark on the body to colour in clothing. If the elf seems too long, secateurs can be used to trim off the end. Now it's time to name the elves and use them in all manner of imaginative play!

Endings

Once the children have finished playing, you might like to talk more about elves. What do the children know about them? The idea of elves seems to have emerged centuries ago in Norse mythology, and since then elves have appeared in different guises in many different stories, such as J.R.R. Tolkien's *The Lord of the Rings*. In Iceland, even today, elves known as *huldufólk* are thought to make their homes in rocks. The belief is so strong that roads have been rerouted to avoid the homes! The elves are friendly but must be treated with respect – or else! There are stories about road-building machines mysteriously breaking down near the elf territories . . .

WINTER'S WEB

On a winter woodland walk, have you ever come across beads of dew glistening like jewels on a spider's web? Leafless trees frame these architectural wonders perfectly, and give us a chance to see how intricate these designs are and how difficult it would be for a passing insect to escape their sticky, threadlike strings. Winter's Web is a game in which ropes like giant spider threads are woven between trees for willing players to move through without touching them. Lots of excitement and enthusiasm are triggered as the children hone agile moves to evade capture by the ropes – a perfect activity to tune into what's around outside while having fun in these colder winter months.

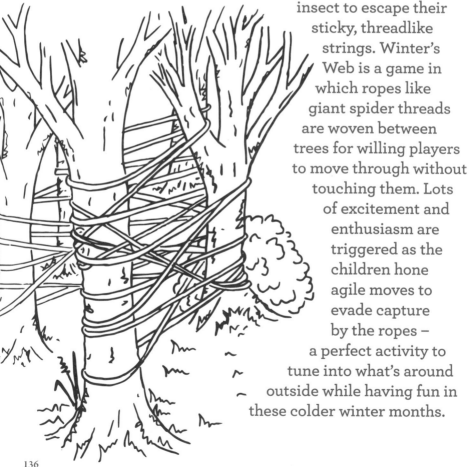

The game involves lots of physical movement as the players twist
and turn through the web. As they design and build the web (with
help, if needed), fine motor skills and knot tying come into play,
while thoughts turn to spiders and their prey. Rushing through can
cost a "life" so patience, focus and perseverance are required. It's
a great way of learning to deal with frustration, as they get caught
in the web. All the cheering and encouragement deepen a sense
of empathy and community, and above all, this game is full of
laughter, comical moves and lots of banter – we love it!

Get ready

Choose an area in the woods where you can weave and tie cord
around trees to create a giant spider's web – the more intricate the
better. Lots of spiders' webs hang vertically, but this web should be

LOCATION	Woodland with lots are trees and potential spider webs is ideal, but any outdoor space with trees to tie rope to can also work
AGE GROUP	3 years +
LEARNING ABOUT ...	⊛ Gross and fine motor skills ⊛ knots ⊛ patience ⊛ focus ⊛ perseverance ⊛ empathy ⊛ community ⊛ self-regulation ⊛ trust ⊛ nature connections ⊛ playfulness
KIT	⇢ 3 x 20m (65ft) lengths of paracord, string or rope (shorter lengths make a simpler web)

challenging horizontally *and* vertically, so the players can move
through it several times in different and unique ways. The children
can have fun designing and building the web, with assistance
from you as needed. For younger children, a simplified structure
(requiring less rope) will lessen potential frustration – in other
words, keep it challenging but do-able.

Get set

Now decide whether children will play one by one or in two
teams racing against each other. We've found that older children
enjoy the latter option, but if you feel this would create a negative
competitive atmosphere, encourage players to have a go against
the web itself. They may want to play against you, especially the
younger ones! Choose whichever version you feel fits your group,
keeping in mind that proceedings should be light-hearted and fun.

Anyone who wants to watch but not play can be elected the rope
buzzer; whenever someone touches the rope, the rope buzzer makes
a buzzing sound, which signals the loss of one of the player's lives.
If no one wants this role, the adults can do it – you'll find everyone's
eyes will be helping you watch out for insects caught in the web!

Go!

Line up in groups or in a single line at a chosen starting point on
the web. Remind the players that they each have three lives. On
each go they have to make it through the web without touching
it with any part of their body. If they touch it, the web buzzes and
they lose a life and must exit the web and join the end of the line,
waiting for another go. It's then the turn of the next person in line.

The challenge, however, gets harder each time. So, the first time you go through, you can use all your limbs to help you duck, twist and balance. But, on the second time through, you can use only three of your limbs to help you. So, for example, you could balance and duck through using both your legs and one arm to steady you, or alternatively both your arms and one leg. On the last go through, you're down to only two limbs at a time. This is where the game becomes the most fun – expect some very creative contortions! If older children seem to be finding it too easy, you can always set a time limit to add an extra element to the challenge.

Let the game begin: three, two, one – go! Keep going until everyone has been through three times. Get ready for lots of cheering, laughter and debating about what works best! And of course, if the children haven't already made you, you can always have a go!

Endings

You could talk through all the different tactics the children employed, then ask them whether they can think of any way to improve the web. Which parts of constructing the web were easy and which were hard? Does this make them think about how clever a spider's web is? The web is a spider's lifeline, for catching food as well as a home. Webs can catch all sorts of invertebrates that have the misfortune of crawling or flying into the sticky trap, including flies and mosquitoes. In this way, spiders play an important role in the ecosystem by controlling insect numbers, and they in turn provide a food source for other species, such as birds, toads, shrews and hedgehogs. Weight for weight, a spider's silk is tougher than steel! How amazing is that?

COMPASS TREASURE HUNT

Our Forest School groups just love a treasure hunt! This is another energetic activity to keep everyone warm when they're outside in winter, and if the treasure is food (which it often is on our hunts), a treat to eat makes the natural space feel welcoming, as well as providing a handy energetic boost. As soon as we announce that a Compass Treasure Hunt is on, the children come running, jumping up and down, all eager to hold the compass and lead the way!

This activity teaches children how to use a compass (a valuable survival tool!) and look closely at the landscape for clues, increasing their sense of independence and self-reliance and connections to nature. Deciding who will hold the compass when, and who might read the bearings, encourages communication, negotiation, maths and teamwork. Looking for treasure always means excitement, laughs and light-hearted

Direction-of-travel arrow

Index line

Magnetized needle

Bezel, marked with degrees

LOCATION	Spacious woodland with lots of landmarks is ideal, but other natural spaces can work too
AGE GROUP	6 years +
LEARNING ABOUT ...	❀ Communication ❀ negotiation ❀ teamwork ❀ trust ❀ maths ❀ physics ❀ independence ❀ self-reliance ❀ nature connections
KIT	⇾ Treasure and treasure box (for example, treats in a waterproof container) ⇾ Pen (or permanent marker pens if using laminated paper) — ⇾ Brightly coloured paper for clues (laminated paper for wet days) ⇾ A compass (or a few compasses for a large group)
OPTIONAL	⇾ Cellophane, plastic wrap or equivalent to wrap clues in if rain is likely and clues are not laminated

pranks, some of them from nature itself. On one occasion, we had finally come across the hidey hole where a box of marshmallows was hidden. We pulled out the treasure box with eager anticipation – everyone keen to get at the contents – only to find that they had already been eaten! We couldn't believe our eyes and the whole group burst out laughing. Had a cheeky squirrel spied the box's burial? Or was the culprit a passing dog who couldn't believe its luck? The mystery remains to this day. Luckily, we had some spare marshmallows!

Get ready

To set up the treasure hunt, hide the treasure somewhere that can be seen from a distance, such as in a tree (at a child-friendly height). From here, you are now going to lay clues along the treasure-hunt route, working backward so you end up at the start.

Look around and choose another landmark that you can see – a fallen tree or a bench, for example. Now pace out your steps to this new landmark, counting one pace every time your right foot lands. Once you arrive at your landmark, write down the number of paces on a clue card. Then, take a reading on your compass from where you are standing to the treasure. To do this, face the treasure location, hold the compass straight at stomach height and line up the fixed direction-of-travel arrow with the treasure location landmark. Twist the bezel to line up the floating magnetized needle with N (north) on the dial, then read the co-ordinates (degrees) given at the index line on the compass and write these down on the clue card. Hide this clue card in the first landmark area. Now look for a new landmark and repeat until you find yourself back at base camp. This last clue card will be the first clue to give to the group.

Get set

Show everyone the parts of the compass (see illustration on page 140) and explain how it works. Hand them the first clue card with the co-ordinates and number of paces needed to find the next clue. To work out how to get to the next clue card, the children will use the compass to line up the index line to the degrees given on the clue card. Once they've done this, they need to line up the floating magnetized needle with N. Now they need to follow where the direction-of-travel arrow is pointing for the number of paces given on the clue card to reach the next clue. Let them know how many clues there are in total.

Go!

Let the children head off on the hunt, reminding them to share the compass if they need to. Gently guide them if they accidentally head off in the wrong direction and provide hints if they are becoming frustrated in their search for the next clue. When the treasure is discovered, share out the bounty amidst cheers of celebration for an amazing job well done!

> **TRY THIS!**
> If just one adult lays the trail, the others can truly join in with the children and will be seen by as part of the team, rather than as someone separate with all the knowledge.

Endings

Did the children enjoy the hunt and the treasure? What about using a compass, was that easy or confusing? Compasses are fantastic tools. This treasure hunt is a first step in becoming familiar with a compass, so now might be a good time to talk more about how it can be used. For example, the floating magnetized needle always points not to the true North Pole (a geographical location) but to the magnetic North Pole (which can shift due to magnetic changes in the Earth's core). Compasses also have an orienting arrow, which is usually large and outlined inside the bevel. Using an up-to-date map with marked declination bearings, you can adjust this orienting arrow (where you are) to face true north . . . handy for survival if hiking in the mountains!

ANIMAL TRACK CASTS

It's winter: the trees are bare and vegetation has died down. The view across the landscape has opened up, making it easier for shy animals to see you coming and dart out of sight. With a little detective work, however, you will be able to discover which creatures live nearby. And you might be surprised by what you find!

This is a great activity for winter, when there's plenty of mud to investigate. It makes what can feel like a barren season seem full of adventure and life, even if this is hidden from view! Hunting for tracks involves finding the right conditions on the ground, then locating and identifying prints; doing this requires focus, perseverance and an understanding of the way local animals move and live, connecting the children to the natural environment. Creating a plaster of Paris cast to preserve the track is a challenging part of the activity, requiring concentration, patience and listening skills, and the end result is a lasting memento of their time outside.

TRY THIS!
Putting some apples out overnight near a muddy spot like a river bank might encourage animals to visit and leave their tracks for casting the next day.

When we have made casts with our Forest School groups, the children have always been bursting with questions and ideas about what they might find and where. They are fascinated by the process in which liquid plaster of Paris hardens into a fantastic sculpture of an animal print that can be lifted from the ground and taken home to be treasured and shared with others.

LOCATION	Muddy or silty locations show the tracks best
AGE GROUP	4 years +
LEARNING ABOUT ...	❀ Being healthy and active ❀ focus ❀ perseverance ❀ nature connections ❀ identification skills ❀ sharing ❀ planning ❀ measuring ❀ patience ❀ listening skills ❀ concentration ❀ transferable skills and ideas

KIT	
⇀ Hobby/craft plaster of Paris	person)
⇀ Water bottle with water (enough to mix the plaster)	⇀ Track identification pocket book or app
	⇀ An old spoon
	⇀ Newspaper
⇀ Zip-lock plastic bags for plaster (one per	⇀ Bag to carry casts
	⇀ Rubbish bags

OPTIONAL	⇀ Bowl or container, zip-lock bags for water, 30 x 13 cm (12 x 5in) strips of card (e.g. cut from old cereal boxes), sticky tape/stapler, Vaseline, disposable vinyl gloves (for younger children), paper clips (one per person), trowel

Get ready

We find it easier to measure out the water into a bottle and the plaster of Paris into zip-lock bags before we head out. The ratio for your mix will be shown on the plaster of Paris packet but is usually two parts plaster to one part water. Alternatively, measure out the plaster of Paris on site into a mixing bowl. If there is a nearby water source, you could collect the required water in an empty zip-lock bag (which is lighter than carrying it in a bottle).

Get set

Show some pictures of animal tracks that might be found. If the track is paw-shaped with four to five toes, it probably belongs to a mammal, like a dog, or, if it's small, a squirrel. Two parallel horn-shaped tracks might be a deer, while birds leave small fork-shaped tracks.

Go!

Now start hunting for tracks! Try looking next to water (even puddles), where there will be mud and animals may come to drink. Once you have found a track, clear out any leaves and twigs. Now, using the mud, build a sturdy dam about 2.5cm (1in) high all around the print to hold in the plaster. Alternatively, make a dam using cardboard strips by slightly overlapping the ends and joining them together with a stapler or tape (staple or tape both inside and out). Place it over the track and push it up to 2.5cm (1in) into the ground. A smear of Vaseline around the inside of the cardboard can help later to ease the set cast out.

TRY THIS!
After about 15 minutes, when the cast has started to set but is still soft, you can use a stick to scratch out a name, date or whatever you like in the plaster – once set it will remain there to be read in the future

Pour the water into the plaster of Paris. If using a zip-lock bag, close the zip and mix the plaster together by slowly squeezing the bag. If using a bowl (or if any lumps form in the bag), gently mix to a smooth paste (like pancake batter) with a stick or spoon. Don't stir too vigorously, as air bubbles will take detail away from the cast. Younger children can wear vinyl gloves to avoid getting plaster on their hands.

Pour the plaster to one side of the track and let it slowly run into the track, filling the dam area. Smooth out the surface with the back of a spoon. You could now set a bent paper clip in the plaster and use it later to hang up your cast. Leave to set for at least 30 minutes, then touch to see if it is hard (if it is still soft, dig away the dam or remove the cardboard and leave for roughly 15 minutes more). While waiting for the cast to dry, look for more tracks. If hard, peel off the cardboard or use a stick or a trowel to remove 10–13 cm (4–5in) of mud from the outside of the cast. Next, dig away the mud from below the cast and carefully lift it up with your fingers (not the trowel or stick). If there is resistance, clear away more mud until the cast comes away easily. The cast will still be fragile, so have a good look and then wrap it up in newspaper to take it home to dry completely for one more day to ensure it is fully set. Then you can wash away any mud that's left. You will now have a wonderful animal track to hang on the wall, paint or simply admire!

Endings

Have a look at all the wonderful animal casts. Ask the children how they felt looking for tracks. Did they find anything unexpected? Other than for casting, can they think of any reason why people would look for animal tracks? Our hunter-gatherer ancestors would have looked for tracks to find food. Today, checking tracks is important for wildlife biologists, as they can tell you a lot about an animal's lifestyle and how we might be able to help it – for example, where and how it lives and where it travels, alone or in a group.

HIGH TARP SHELTER

Shelter is an essential requirement for human survival. When children build a shelter, they create a place of their own to feel safe and protected from the elements. It's somewhere to call home for a short while, where everyone can gather to share jokes and stories and be creative, enjoying a sense of belonging.

The high shelter described here is made from tarps suspended from tree branches, providing cover for a whole group to sit and move around under, with space for a warming fire that will make those wintery days feel cosy and inviting. There are various different types of tarp available (see opposite); we like DD tarps as they are light, easy to carry and quick to put up, which makes all the difference in bad weather. Bear in mind, if you are planning a fire, that most tarps, although not very flammable, will burn if exposed to open flames. Fire retardant tarps (rated FR) will not continue to burn after the source of the flame has been removed. Canvas tarps offer more fire resistance but are much heavier to carry.

Working out how much cord is needed, how to position the tarps and how to tie the knots are all fun, practical ways of learning about maths, physics and communication. As the children work to check ground conditions and assess which branches are suitable to use as support points and other risks, they develop independence, become bonded as a group and immersed in the natural world that surrounds them. And when the shelter is complete, the builders enjoy feelings of achievement and confidence in their own abilities.

LOCATION	Woodland with trees to support the tarp set-up; if having a fire, a site that allows their use is ideal
AGE GROUP	6 years +
LEARNING ABOUT ...	✿ Risk assessment and management ✿ independence ✿ self-reliance ✿ nature connections ✿ physics ✿ mathematics ✿ communication ✿ listening skills ✿ teamwork ✿ confidence ✿ empathy ✿ community ✿ knots
KIT	⇾ Two 4 x 4m (13 x 13ft) DD tarps (good to shelter 12), but number and size depends on the size of your group. Tarps come in different materials such as plastic, canvas or coated waterproof fabrics. DD tarps are versatile, light, pack away neatly and come in many colours. ⇾ 50–100m (55–110yd) spool of paracord (to cover future use, too). We prefer paracord as it's strong, easy to use and available in bright colours (ideal on dark wintry days to help avoid trip hazards). You could also use string, bank line or rope to tie up the tarps. ⇾ Scissors
OPTIONAL	⇾ Groundsheets, telescopic walking poles, 4 x tent pegs (perhaps homemade wooden ones, see page 102), mallet/rubber hammer, gardening gloves (for holding peg), camp fire (see page 89) plus fire safety kit (see page 15), additional tarp to block wind, tea-making kit

Get ready

These instructions are for a shelter using two 4 x 4m (13 x 13ft) tarps (adjust accordingly for one tarp). For a high tarp shelter, you will need two trees with branches at about 2m (7ft) high to support the paracord ridgeline at either end (see illustration on page 155). One side of each tarp will be secured to this ridgeline, with the other side of each tarp tensioned and attached to two further trees. So you'll need six trees in total with space enough in between for the tarps to be spread out. (If you struggle finding all these trees, walking poles can be used to secure the corners of the tarp that are opposite the ridgeline.)

Invite the children to look for the ideal set-up. Trees should not have any visible rot, damage or dead hanging branches that could fall on the shelter or any fungus indicating disease. Ideally the ground will be flattish, as this is better for sitting on and pools of water are less likely to gather if it's raining, as well as free from litter and trip hazards. If necessary, show them what 4 x 4m (13 x 13ft) looks like on the ground by pacing it out. The trees need to be slightly wider apart than this. If you are planning on having a fire, now is also the time to think about wind direction, it's best to have the lower sides of the shelter (the sides away from the ridgeline) facing the wind to limit it reaching the fire.

Get set

Once a safe and suitable spot has been found, show everyone the cord and the tarps, including the eyelets (through which cord is threaded to secure the shelter along the ridgeline and to trees or pegs) plus guylines, if the tarps have them.

Take out the cord and lay it down between the ridgeline support trees. This cord needs to be long enough to accommodate your tarps, to go over a high branch and wrap at least a couple of times around the trees at either end. On the ground, line up the tarps on either side of the ridgeline cord.

Go!

To attach the tarps to the ridgeline using Prusik and bow knots Demonstrate how to use Prusik knots to attach the tarps to the ridgeline. Take a 70cm (28in) piece of cord and fold in half, lining up the ends. Place the looped end under the ridgeline, pull it up and wrap it around the ridgeline by threading the ends through the loop.

Wrap it under and around the ridgeline again. Do this 3–4 times, keeping each turn neatly lined up against each other. On the final wrap, pass the free ends back through the loop and pull tight. The Prusik knot is now in place.

To attach the loose ends of the Prusik knot cord to the tarp eyelets, use a simple bow knot (which is also a quick-release knot). If you are planning a fire, aim to leave around 7cm (2¾in) between the Prusik knot on the ridgeline and the tarp eyelet – this will give a gap for the smoke to exit.

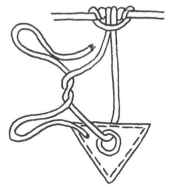

151

The children may be familiar with a simple bow knot from tying shoe laces. Pass one of the two ends of cord hanging from the Prusik knot through the eyelet on the tarp, then cross the two ends of cord over each other to form a cross shape and pass the front piece underneath the back of the cross and through to the front. Form each of the two loose ends of the cord into a loop. Pass the first loop (it does not matter which) across the second, then behind and through the hole formed at the base of the loops.

Pull the two loops tight to secure. To undo the tarp, pull the loose working ends of the bow knot to free the knot, then loosen the tension on the Prusik knot and unwind the cord. Now let the children tie the tarp to the ridgeline while it is still on the floor. Once done, ask them to use the Prusik knots to pull the tarp taut along the ridgeline and leave in place. Use the same method to attach the second tarp to the ridgeline.

Throwing the cord of the ridgeline Discuss with the group the best branches on the chosen trees to attach the ridgeline to (at least 2m/7ft up). Once chosen, both ends of the cord need to be thrown over each of these branches. This may take a few goes!

Anchoring the ridgeline using a timber hitch Once over the first branch, anchor the cord to the tree using a version of the

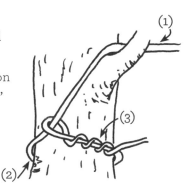

timber hitch. We will call the section of cord attached to the tarps and dangling over the branch the "standing end" (1), and the section of cord we will be moving the "working end" (allow at least 90cm/35in here to make the knot). Get someone to hold the furthest end of the standing end tight. Whoever is holding the working end now pulls on the cord, bringing it down to a comfortable height, and wraps it around the back of the tree (2). Once around the tree, throw the loose working end over the standing end toward the trunk (this standing end will now be coming down at an angle from the branch to the tree). Now loop the working end (that is now around the trunk) 3–4 times around itself (3). Pull and tighten the knot against the tree. (To release it, slacken the line and unloop the knot.)

Tensioning the ridgeline Ask the children to throw the other end of the ridgeline cord over the second chosen high branch, then pull on the cord to tighten the ridgeline and raise the tarps.

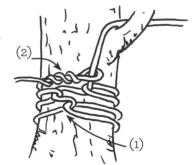

To tension the ridgeline in place, repeat the version of the timber hitch process. This time, however, pull the working end slightly lower down and when you take the working end under the standing end, do not thread the working end around itself. Instead, ask the children to wrap the cord around the back of the tree, again pulling tight and tensioning the line as they go (1).

The working end should again be passed over and under the standing line and brought back around the tree. You can keep repeating this process until you feel the ridgeline is tensioned enough, then finish off the timber hitch as before, looping the working end several times around itself (2, previous page).

Tensioning the tarps using an overhand knot and timber hitch knot Now the two dangling corners of each tarp each need to be attached to trees. If guylines are already attached to the eyelets, use these. If not, cut pieces of cord (two per tarp) to the desired length, enough to do both an overhand and a timber hitch knot.

Tie one end of the cut cord to the eyelet using a simple overhand knot: fold roughly 13cm (5in) of one end of the cord over and make a loop, then thread the folded end through the loop and pull tight; this creates a fixed loop at the end. Now pass the loop through the eyelet. Tuck the other single end of cord through the loop and pull tight. Tie the cord or the guyline to a tree using a timber hitch, tying the tarp corners below the ridgeline to aid rainwater run-off. Repeat, securing both corners of each tarp.

If you are finding it difficult to find suitable trees, telescopic walking poles work well as an alternative. Extend to the desired height then, close to the eyelet, wrap the paracord or guyline twice around the top of walking pole handle. Pull the cord tight to the ground and use a peg to secure into place.

The shelter is now ready to be furnished! You can put groundsheets down to sit on, or perhaps use logs. Building a fire under the tallest part of the shelter will make it really cosy (for the basics of setting a fire, see page 89). The smoke should drift through the gaps in the tarp along the ridgeline, but keep the fire small (if a tarp feels hot to the touch, the fire is too close). To help prevent burning holes in the tarp, avoid timber, such as resinous softwoods, that spits out embers – hardwoods like oak burn in a more controlled way. If you are planning a fire, it can be useful to drape another tarp at the windward side of the set-up to completely block the wind from reaching the fire.

Endings

Let everyone know what a fantastic, essential job they did in putting up the shelter. How do they feel now they have made a temporary home in the woods? Could they do it again? Talk through any parts they may have found tricky or hard. If it was the knots, would they like to practise them some more? It can be interesting to talk more about shelter, and how early humans used to make a home in trees, caves or cliffs. What other materials in the woods could be used for building a shelter today?

WINTER DAY OUT

With the right kit, a winter's day out in nature can be truly uplifting. The crisp air refreshes lungs and clears minds, and with no artificial heating or lights around, bodies start to tune into the season. The landscape takes on a different feel at this time of year – everything is still and peaceful. The trees are bare and reveal their magical silhouettes as each branch stretches out across the skyline. It feels right to follow nature's lead and slow down, taking in the new view. Everything as it should be in this wonderful season.

Here is a guide for a fantastic winter's day out: a game for fun, food and drink with seasonal spices, and charcoal made on a camp fire to draw the magical wintry scene. Charcoal is created when you char wood, depriving it of oxygen to leave a dark soot-like residue. It has many uses, the most common being as a fuel, but it is also popular with artists, who love to draw with charcoal, leaving light or intensely black marks, smudges or defined lines. As it can be easily erased, it is the ideal tool to experiment with, sparking creativity especially when you've made it yourself. Sharing art also builds communication, trust and community. And making the charcoal itself offers so much: forging links to nature through identifying the right wood, teaching how to assess and manage risk when using tools and fire, developing confidence, independence and patience – all this raising self-esteem.

Zip Zap Boing is perfect for playing under a high tarp shelter (see page 148) in bad weather, as players stand in one spot while

LOCATION	Woodland that allows fires and has softwoods
AGE GROUP	4 years +
LEARNING ABOUT ...	✿ Tree identification ✿ tool and fire use ✿ risk management and assessment ✿ nature connections ✿ independence ✿ confidence ✿ self-esteem ✿ pride ✿ planning ✿ patience ✿ creativity ✿ imagination ✿ trust ✿ community ✿ self-regulation ✿ transfer of learning ✿ communication ✿ concentration ✿ focus ✿ memory ✿ reflexes ✿ hygiene ✿ empathy
FLOW OF THE DAY	See page 45

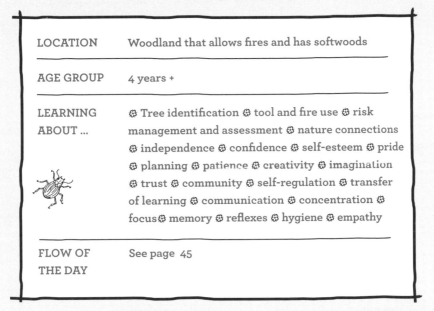

getting lots of warming exercise jumping up and down. It's a game that builds concentration, memory and quick reflexes, and a great ice-breaker, too. You also have to rely on yourself, helping to build confidence, and the game provides a safe space to work through any disappointment, developing self-regulation skills.

There is nothing quite like cooking your own food on a camp fire and then eating it – our Forest School groups just love it, and it's a great way of teaching skills relating to food preparation and fire safety that in turn can develop patience, confidence, focus and communication, while pride, empathy and a sense of community are formed through sharing the space and food. Here, bread, in the form of dampers, is roasted over the fire, giving off that freshly baked aroma. To wash down the dampers, there's hot spiced apple juice, which also fills the air with a wonderful Christmassy scent.

Activity 1: CHARCOAL PENCILS

Get ready

You'll need to make a fire to make the charcoal and for cooking and generally keeping warm on what is sure to be a cold day. See pages 89 and 121 for fire set-up ideas. Before you start, run through the fire safey rules (see page 15).

Get set

Everyone hunts for wood to make the charcoal, looking for sticks about 15cm (6in) long (they need to fit in the container) and ranging in width from the thickness of a pencil to that of an adult's

KIT	
→ Camp fire (see page 89) and fire safety kit (see page 15)	on group size (e.g. coffee/cookie tins or a clean paint can)
→ Potato peelers	→ Cartridge or pastel paper
→ Hammer	→ Clipboards or something similar to place paper on (one per person)
→ Nail	
→ Gardening gloves	
→ Large tongs	
→ Metal container with tight-fitting lid, size dependent	→ Kneaded erasers
	→ Secateurs

OPTIONAL	
→ Sticks for making charcoal – ideally softwood such as willow/pine (if not available locally), wire and wire cutters, wet wipes, screwdriver, tarp/camping chairs to sit on, paper towels, strong aluminium foil, fire bowl	

thumb. If they're too small or thin, the charcoal sticks can become brittle when used. Any wood will do, but two-year-old softwood such as willow or pine is ideal. Preferably, you want sticks that are not too green (they hold more moisture so will take longer to burn), so try to find them on the forest floor, avoiding rotten or mouldy wood. If cutting fresh twigs, remember to ask the landowner's permission first. Cut from the tips of the branches using secateurs following safety procedures as you go (see pages 12–14) The wood will shrink as it turns to charcoal, so gather enough to really pack the tin full.

Once you have your sticks, the bark needs to be peeled away using potato peelers, as it doesn't burn down to charcoal too well. Demonstrate how to use these safely (see pages 12–14), then everyone can sit around the fire to keep warm as they peel their sticks (assist if needed).

TRY THIS!
If you don't have a suitable tin, use four or more well-sealed layers of strong tin foil to wrap 5–6 sticks on coals that have died down.

Holes need to be punched in the lid of the tin to allow the wood gasses to escape as the tin and wood heat up. To punch the holes, place the lid on a hard surface such as a stump and use the hammer to lightly tap the nail to create a hole. Repeat until you have three evenly spaced holes. If a child is doing this, get them to put a glove on the hand that is holding the nail. (If there are more than three who want to punch the holes, choosing to complete this section yourself helps to avoid disputes!)

Now everyone places their peeled sticks in the tin and the lid is put on. If the lid seems loose, you can wire it shut to prevent it popping open. Remind everyone that this is a team effort – their particular stick will be in with all the others, so it may be difficult to locate once it's ready. If so, each piece of charcoal will be shared out randomly amongst the group.

Go!

The fire needs to be hot, so add more wood if necessary and wait until it's all burning. Then, with tongs and fire-resistant gloves, place the tin in the hot fire, making sure it's covered by flames. You can turn the tin after 20 minutes if you think the heat needs to be distributed more evenly. As the tin heats up, you will see a jet of smoke coming out of the vent holes as the gases in the wood are being released. Because there is no oxygen in the tin, the wood will char but not burn. When it gets really hot, the smoke can catch fire, which will look like a small flame-thrower coming out of the holes. When the smoke and flames stop, the charcoal is done. This is usually after 45 minutes to an hour – so why not play Zip Zap Boing (page 162) while you wait?

When the charcoal is ready, remove the tin from the fire with tongs and fire-resistant gloves. Put it somewhere safe, where no one will be able to accidentally touch it. To keep out any oxygen, place a pebble over each hole (or a damp paper towel if you have it). Leave to cool down for at least 10 minutes or until safe to touch. If using a container such as a paint can, open with a screwdriver or a flat rock.

Once cold, the charcoal is ready to use on the cartridge or pastel paper. Give each child a clipboard to rest their paper on for drawing. Mistakes can be fixed with a kneaded eraser. You may want to wait until nearer the end of the day, after everyone has eaten, to create some fabulous charcoal drawings – it's up to you, but once complete admire each work of art!

Endings

Burning wood in this way leaves only carbon, which is the charcoal! Look at how amazing it is – how black the wood is and how much it has all shrunk! See how it seems much more brittle and easy to snap. How do the children feel now that they have made their very own artist's charcoal, as good as any they would find in a shop? Can they think of any other uses for charcoal? Charcoal is valuable – it's used for cooking (when you have a barbecue, for example) and it's also used as a fuel, creating intense heat to melt metals in foundries. It is ground up to make black pigment, used to filter air and water, and, medically, can help to extract swallowed poison from the body. And let's not forget that it's used in the making of black powder – otherwise known as gunpowder. When everyone has created a work of art, talk through why each artist chose to draw what they did and what it means to them.

Activity 2: ZIP ZAP BOING

Get ready

In this game everyone stands in a circle, throwing an imaginary ball from person to person, along with a gesture and a word: Zip, Zap or Boing. The aim of the game is to try and close the circle by catching someone out when they forget what to do or hesitate. Each game will last for ten minutes.

GESTURES AND WORDS:

Zip is when you pass the imaginary ball to someone either side of you, left or right, call out "Zip!" and hold your hands out as if passing them the ball. The receiver can then respond with a Zip, a Zap or a Boing.

Zap is when you pass across the circle. It can be to anyone except someone to your left or right. When passing the ball across the circle, call out "Zap!" and throw the imaginary ball. Maintain eye contact with the receiver, so they are sure you mean them. This player may now respond with a Zip, Zap or Boing.

Boing If you don't wish to receive the ball, jump up in the air facing the person who aimed at you and, with your hands reaching high, call out "Boing". Now it's their turn again to Zip or Zap someone else (but they cannot Boing). Remember to keep the game fast!

| KIT | → Watch or timer on phone |

Get set

Ask who would like to start. If there is only one volunteer, start with them; otherwise choose someone at random. Set your timer for ten minutes, then begin the countdown: three, two, one . . .

Go!

The starting player calls out "Zip" (to pass the ball either side of them) or "Zap" (to pass the ball across the circle). The receiver can then do a Zip or a Zap – or a Boing to bounce the ball back to the first player. If anyone forgets what to do or hesitates for too long (say, two seconds max for older kids – increase slightly for younger kids, especially while new to the game), they are out for this round. The game carries on until there are only three players remaining or ten minutes has elapsed. Then, if you wish to, you can play another round. Expect lots of muddled-up words and fits of laughter. Our favourite so far has been someone throwing a "Bap" – a mix of "Boing" and "Zap – whereupon the receiver (quick to pick up on the muddle) ate it!

Endings

Did everyone enjoy the game? Talk through how it feels to make mistakes (especially if anyone looks upset at not being one of the final players) and how we all make mistakes at one time or another, but that it's ok as we can learn from them. Would they like to play again? Or, after all that jumping around, and with the fire now burning down to cooking coals, what about some food . . . ?

Activity 3: DAMPERS AND MULLED APPLE JUICE

DAMPERS

Get ready

It's time to prepare
the dampers, ready to
cook on the fire once
it has burned down to coals.
Each child needs to find a long,
thin stick (roughly the length of their
forearm to the end of their hand and as thick as an adult's thumb).
When they have their sticks and washed hands, it can be helpful to
make an example of a damper for everyone to see and feel, so they
know what they are aiming for.

Get set

To make the damper mix, put roughly 90g (3¼oz) self-raising flour
in a plastic bowl, then slowly add approximately
30ml (2 tbsp) water and mix together with
a spoon. When combined, pick up the
dough and knead it between your
hands. It should feel a bit like pizza
dough – if you rub it and it shines
you know it's good to go. This should
be enough for two dampers. Pass it
around the group and let everyone
see how it feels. Now its the turn of

> **TRY THIS!**
> If you have no
> plastic mixing bowls,
> old takeaway cartons are
> great for mixing
> dampers in.

KIT To make the dampers:	→ Self-raising flour (1kg/2¼lb bag works well for 12 large rolls) → 1 litre (2 pints) water → Knives for spreads	→ Spoons, small plastic mixing bowls (one per person) → Aluminium foil → Butter and jam (or other spread)
To make the mulled apple juice:	→ Sharp knife → Apple juice (enough for group) → For every litre (34fl oz) apple juice, you'll need: 1 cinnamon stick 2 cloves	Peel and juice of one orange 2 star anise → Fireproof saucepan → Cups (one per person and one extra to serve) → Rubbish bag
OPTIONAL	→ Long sticks (if fallen ones not available), weighing scales, measuring jug, wet wipes, 3–4 thin slices of washed unpeeled ginger root	

everyone else. Older children can do all this themselves; younger kids may need help, so assist as needed.

Go!

Now it's time to cook the dampers. To keep the dough clean and prevent the stick from burning, each baker needs to wrap a piece of aluminium foil (long enough to accomodate the dough) around the end of the stick (the part that will be placed over the fire).

The bakers need to break the dough into two pieces and set one aside to cook later, rolling the other into a sausage shape between their hands. Then, starting at the top of the aluminium foil, they can twist the damper around the stick, squeezing it on as they go to make sure it's secure.

TRY THIS!
If in a large group, make sure everyone has a safe space around the fire to cook. If it becomes crowded, take the baking in turns (four at a time is a good number).

Now, kneeling on one leg outside of the fire safety zone (see page 15), which is the safest position to be in (allowing them to move away from the fire quickly if needed), the bakers place the damper over the fire coals to cook, turning as needed to cook all the way round. And no waving sticks in the air, in and out of the fire or poking neighbours! Each damper should take between 15–20 minutes to cook. When it's done, the bakers can carefully move the damper stick away from the fire and let it cool, before removing it from the stick and adding their choice of spread. If they are still hungry, they can cook their second damper. The best bread ever!

MULLED APPLE JUICE

Get ready

Now it's time for the children (assist where needed) to make the mulled apple juice. Gather all the ingredients, wash the orange and cut it in two.

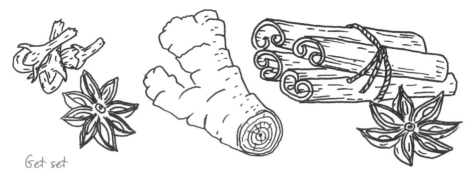

Get set

Pour the apple juice into the saucepan and add the cinnamon, cloves, star anise and ginger (if using). Squeeze the juice from the oranges into the pan and add half of the peel.

Go!

Using fire-resistant gloves, place the mulled apple juice on the coals to cook. It should only take a few minutes to come to the boil. Take it off the fire (again wearing fire-resistant gloves) and leave it to cool to drinking temperature and to allow the spices to infuse. When ready, use one of the cups to ladle out a tasty cupful for everyone to try. Perfect to wash down the damper and fill the air with the aroma of Christmas!

Endings

Ask everyone if they enjoyed sharing and eating the camp-fire food they made by themselves. Did they find preparing the food and fire easy or difficult and why? Would they feel confident to cook again? Can they think of any other flavours to add to the dampers or juice? Now they are warm, settled and full of food, it may (if you haven't done this already) be the ideal time for a charcoal drawing; perhaps a wintry scene, a feeling expressed on paper, or a tree-bark rubbing. A creative end to a wonderful winter day out!

ACKNOWLEDGEMENTS

We want to thank:

Our son Theo, aged 7, for his generosity and support to travel the Forest School journey with us, always bringing new inspiration, a love of nature, curiosity, courage and endless laughs!

The Watkins team, for their hard work.

Ruth Peel, for a shared belief in the Forest School ethos.

And all our fantastic Forest School groups, who have taught us so much.

FOREST FRIENDS by Theo

Kizzie

Theo

Indie

Freya the cat

Flick the cat

PLAY THE FOREST SCHOOL WAY

This bestselling book will get kids outside, making and building in the real world (instead of on a computer screen!). Aimed at children aged 3–11, and offering plenty of ideas for groups as well as for just one or two children, the activities provide fantastic opportunities for family time and days out, whether your local woodland is a forest or a strip of trees along the edge of an urban park.

This was the first book to share Forest School games, crafts and skill-building activities with families and friends. Its magical illustrations and simple instructions will draw children easily into a world of wonder and encourage them to fall in love with outdoor play.

Find out more about Jane Worroll and Peter Houghton's Forest School via
email: theforestschoolway@gmail.com
website: www.playtheforestschoolway.com
 facebook.com/theforestschoolway